Managing Violence in Schools

A Whole-School Approach to Best Practice

Helen Cowie and Dawn Jennifer

P·C·P
Paul Chapman
Publishing

First published 2007

 Paul Chapman Publishing
A SAGE Publications Company
1 Oliver's Yard
55 City Road
London EC1Y 1SP

SAGE Publications Inc
2455 Teller Road
Thousand Oaks, California 91320

SAGE Publications India Pvt Ltd
B 1/I 1 Mohan Cooperative Industrial Area
Mathura Road, Post Bag 7
New Delhi 110 044

SAGE Publications Asia-Pacific Pte Ltd
33 Pekin Street #02–01
Far East Square
Singapore 048763

Library of Congress Control Number: 2007926221

British Library in Publication Data
A catalogue record for this book is available from
the British Library

ISBN 978-1-4129-3439-8
ISBN 978-1-4129-3440-4 (pbk)

Typeset by Dorwyn, Wells, Somerset
Printed in Great Britain by T.J. International, Padstow, Cornwall
Printed on paper from sustainable resources

To Corrie, Isabel and Haruki (HC)
To Flora, Alex and Dave (DJ)

Contents

List of Tables, Boxes and Case studies

List of Activities, Activity Handouts and Figures

Acknowledgements

ABC Training Services

Anthony Daly

Nicky Hutson

Flora Jennifer-Burchell who supplied the illustrations on pp. 129-31

Jill Knell

Carrie Anne Myers

Julie Shaughnessy

Steve Wooldridge

British Psychological Society

Council of Europe

World Health Organization

1 | Introduction

> The true measure of a nation's standing is how well it attends to its children – their health and safety, their material security, their education and socialization, and their sense of being loved, valued, and included in the families and societies into which they are born. (UNICEF, 2007: 1)

We are living in an age where violence affects all schools. In a recent survey, Oliver and Candappa (2003) found that half of primary school children and more than one in four of secondary school children in their sample reported that they had been bullied in the previous term. Levels of homophobic bullying remain high (Rivers and Cowie, 2006; YWCA, 2004). Certain children are especially vulnerable to violence, such as children in residential care (Barter et al., 2004), children from gypsy traveller families (Derrington and Kendall, 2004), and children with learning or communication difficulties (Mencap, 2000). Children from minority groups continue to experience direct and indirect bullying of a racist nature.

New forms of violence, such as cyberbullying, are on the increase and have become 'a new arsenal of weapons for violence in schools' (Shariff, 2005: 467). Cyberbullying is a form of covert psychological bullying conveyed through electronic media such as mobile phones, weblogs and websites, or online chatrooms. This disturbing development is particularly pernicious since bullies can remain anonymous by hiding behind screen names and can quickly reach a wide audience of peers. In addition, the victim of cyberbullying can be reached at home and at all hours of the day or night. Bullying of girls by text or email is on the increase, with up to one-fifth of those surveyed claiming to have been sent nasty messages during the past year (Noret and Rivers, 2006). Cyberbullying takes a number of forms that include:

- *text message/phone call bullying*: where someone sends or telephones intimidating or abusive messages to a person's mobile phone;
- *happy slapping*: where individuals or groups make film clips of a person

in a humiliating situation, such as being physically attacked, and these are circulated to a group of peers to embarrass or offend that person;

- *email bullying*: where individuals or groups send unwanted, anonymous messages by email to humiliate or offend a person;
- *chatroom bullying*: where abusive messages are written about or to a person in a web-based chatroom or multi-user domain (MUD) under the disguise of a pseudonym;
- *blogging*: where nasty messages about a person appear on websites such as MySpace and Bebo, or Xangas where people create an online personal profile of people that they do not like.

Shariff points out that, although cyberbullying begins anonymously in virtual space, it has a hugely negative influence on learning and interpersonal relationships in the physical world of school, and is detrimental to its victims, to its perpetrators and to bystanders. The longer it persists, the more bystanders join in, so creating an extremely unpleasant atmosphere at school. Fear of unknown perpetrators of cyberbullying can be totally under-mining for victims. David Knight, a young Canadian who was the victim of cyberbullying throughout his final years at high school, expressed his acute distress every time that he logged on to the Internet as follows: 'Rather than just some people, say 30 in a cafeteria, hearing them all yell insults at you, it's up there for 6 billion people to see. Anyone with a computer can see it' (www.cyberbullying.info/bookcase/shelf1/knight/knight.htm).

What Can Schools Do?

You are not alone in having to face up to these unpleasant statistics. The media remind us frequently of extreme acts of violence that have taken place in schools. Schools are rightly vigilant about such dangers but we must also be aware that media reports can raise levels of fear and panic, resulting in under-researched punitive reactions at the expense of long-term strategies that more effectively build safer school communities. The issue is challenging but, as adults responsible for the young people in our care, we cannot ignore it. Children who engage in violent behaviour – whether as perpetrators, victims or bystanders – are at risk. If unchecked, the perpetrators become insensitive to others' pain and increasingly unaware of the antisocial nature of what they do. These children are significantly more likely than other young people to become adults involved in crime and domestic violence. Children who are victimized often stay silent about their experiences because of shame or fear and, as a result, increasingly view themselves as 'subordinates'. They internalize a sense of low self-esteem and a heavy weight of resentment. In between these two groups lie the bystanders – those who observe the oppression though they do not directly take part. Bystanders are at risk of accepting that violence is 'natural'. Some ignore the problem, becoming 'outsiders' who bear no responsibility for what is happening in their school community. Some assist or reinforce the perpetrators of violence and social exclusion. A few become defenders of the victims and so act morally.

So what can schools do? It is easy to feel powerless to take action. However, the evidence shows us that there is a great deal that schools can do to counteract violence and to promote a culture of non-violent solutions to conflict. The whole-school community approach that we propose here has grown from extensive experience of training and knowledge of best practice in the field, and is grounded in a number of years of collaborative research with expert teams from across Europe. We are especially grateful to colleagues from five other European countries (Spain, Ireland, Norway, Belgium and Bulgaria) with whom we worked on the Violence in Schools Training Action (VISTA) Project (Cowie and Jennifer et al., 2007). Developing the ideas from the VISTA project, the whole-school community approach advocated in this book involves as many members of the whole-school community as possible, including teachers, school management, non-teaching staff members, school nurses, doctors, parents, governors, the local community, external organizations and representatives from wider society as a whole. The aim of our approach is to promote non-violence, improve the climate and ethos of the school, enhance relationships among staff, children and young people and parents, and support the emotional health and well-being of young people, and all adult members of the school community.

The whole-school community approach that we outline in this book will give you the basic skills to create a climate in which teachers and pupils work and learn together in greater harmony than before.

Key Features of the Whole-school Community Approach

The whole-school community approach has many facets. At its core is the concept of individual children relating to family (at home) and their peers (at school) within a community, as part of the wider society. The whole-school community approach addresses school violence as a collective challenge. This unique approach to the issue of school violence involves the entire school community, including children and young people, teachers, school nurses, school management, non-teaching staff members, parents, governors, the local community and external organizations.

The World Health Organization's definition of violence takes account of these interrelating contexts when it defines violence as: 'The intentional use of physical force or power, threatened or actual, against oneself, another person, or against a group or a community, that either results in or has a high likelihood of resulting in injury, death or psychological harm, maldevelopment or deprivation' (WHO, 2002: 5).

You will find risks relating to violence in each of these contexts. For example:

- some children are temperamentally impulsive, may find it hard to manage their feelings and have low tolerance for frustration;
- individual children may come from families where harsh, punitive discipline is the norm;
- the school may be located in a community characterized by poverty, deprivation and crime;
- some children gravitate to aggressive peer groups such as gangs which reinforce violent and antisocial behaviour;
- the media constantly expose children to violence in films, games and cartoons;
- every day in the news we see and read about violent conflict and war.

The more that children are exposed to these risk factors, the more likely they are to resort to violence or to become the victims of violence.

Fortunately, we can counteract the risks by strengthening and developing protective factors which act as buffers against the risks. For example:

- Children can learn how to manage strong emotions.
- Adults can practise consistent, non-violent parenting skills.
- Schools can promote effective ways of dealing with conflicts.
- Communities can build on their strengths to counteract violence.
- There are ways in which we can harness the power of the media to challenge antisocial values.

Through the whole-school community approach that we propose, we aim to develop awareness of the risk factors for violence in each of these contexts and at the same time provide school staff and pupils with the skills to develop protective factors.

School policies to prevent violence need to support learning methods that promote cooperative values and that train pupils in effective communication. Teachers can model this way of relating to one another by fostering cooperative group work in their classrooms. Cooperative group work compares favourably with competitive approaches in that it creates opportunities for pupils to share ideas, to challenge opposing ideas in a constructive way, to negotiate with one another and to learn to help one another. One important outcome is that cooperative group work promotes self-esteem and a sense of positive identity. At the same time, an effective whole-school community approach depends on a shared understanding among the members of the school community of core moral values.

A successful whole-school community approach also reduces the incidence of violent behaviour by enhancing relationships among staff and pupils. In this way, it supports the emotional health, well-being and learning potential of children and young people, and of all adult members of the school community. One facet of this involves the bystanders. Rigby and McLaughlin (2005), in their international research into the nature of the bystander role in school violence, emphasize the importance of helping *all* children to develop more caring attitudes. A greater awareness of the impact of actions on others can lead to the active challenging of bullying behaviour in schools by the youngsters themselves. Teachers can foster these values directly through lessons and indirectly by their own ways of relating to other staff and to their pupils. Furthermore, there is a mass of evidence to indicate that peer support by young people trained to use active listening, empathy, mediation and problem-solving can give help to victims of violence and also contribute to a more caring ethos at school.

These restorative, inclusive approaches create opportunities for adults and children alike to explore the following values:

- respect for others regardless of race, gender, age, nationality, class, sexuality, appearance, political or religious belief, physical or mental ability;
- empathy – a willingness to understand the views of others from their standpoint;
- openness to the opinions and perspectives of others;
- a belief that individuals and groups of people can engage in positive change;
- a belief that conflicts can be resolved peacefully;
- a willingness to negotiate;
- appreciation of and respect for diversity;
- self-esteem – accepting the intrinsic value of oneself;
- commitment to social justice, equality and non-violence.

Quite often the family and community experience of young people does not prepare them with social skills that support such values. So it is important that schools:

- consider ways of helping pupils to understand the approaches that challenge violence;
- provide opportunties for sustained experience of resolving conflicts peacefully;
- promote their own behaviour and practice in ways that model the core values outlined above.

What a Whole-school Community Approach to School Violence Has to Offer

In schools which promote a whole-school community approach to violence the pupils and staff develop the following qualities:

Skill and confidence in
- sharing ideas on conflict resolution;
- learning when to compromise;
- learning how and when to intervene to prevent violence;
- developing a vocabulary of emotions;
- developing self-awareness;
- developing sensitivity to others.

Understanding and knowledge about
- the nature of violence;
- children's rights;
- the nature of diversity;
- testing out ideas on rights and responsibilities;
- the role of the bystander in defusing violence;
- tolerance of a range of perspectives on any issue.

Structuring the Whole-school Community Approach Training Sessions

In this book we offer detailed information on how to train teachers, school management, school nurses, non-teaching staff members, pupils, parents, governors, the local community, external organizations and representatives from the wider society through activities, useful resources and references for further study. The training sessions that we offer are introductory half-day school-based events. Their aim is to:

- explore the nature of school violence and share direct experiences of school violence (Chapter 2);
- help participants deepen their understanding of what a whole-school community approach to school violence involves (Chapter 3);
- prepare for change (Chapter 4);
- carry out a needs analysis of violence unique to the school (Chapter 5);
- offer basic guidance on effective interventions to counteract violence (Chapters 6–9);
- monitor antiviolence approaches through a self-help checklist (Chapter 10).

Each chapter is designed as a training event with tried and tested activities to enable people to practise a range of methods in harmony with the whole-school community approach. This is not an exhaustive guide and it may be that your school decides to buy in trained and experienced facilitators to address particular parts of the issue. You may also choose to alter the order of the training, depending on the particular needs of your school. If you would like further information on evidence that underpins the approach and some supplementary activities, we recommend that you explore the VISTA e-book on www.vista-europe.org (Cowie and Jennifer et al., 2007).

We end this chapter with an overview of how this book is structured with a brief summary of each chapter. We then include a list of suggestions for further reading and a selection of useful websites.

Chapter 2 Understanding School Violence

This chapter considers a multiplicity of definitions of school violence from a range of perspectives, including that of the child. Readers are encouraged to consider how different influences might contribute to the development of violence in schools and give the opportunity in the activities to develop their own definitions of violence through a process of exploration, evaluation and shared discussion. This chapter considers strategies for creating a shared understanding of school bullying and violence. It introduces you to the whole-school community model and identifies key risk and protective factors.

Chapter 3 Working with the Whole-school Community

In this chapter, we build on the shared understanding gained from Chapter 2 in order to understand more deeply what is meant by the whole-school community approach. Specifically, the aim of the chapter is to increase awareness of the relationships among different sections of your school community in order to increase understanding of how to involve all of them in promoting non-violence. The chapter discusses in detail four levels of involvement and illustrates the approach with real-life case studies.

Chapter 4 Preparing for Change

The aim of this chapter is to promote a clear understanding of what we mean by a needs analysis and to enable you to recognize your school's *readiness* to change. We provide detailed guidance on the steps you will need to go through when carrying out a needs analysis, starting with the formation of a working group to oversee the process. The activities in this chapter focus on how to manage a whole-school community needs analysis and how to identify and overcome potential problems.

Chapter 5 Conducting a Needs Analysis

This chapter provides readers with a selection of ideas, tools and resources with which to carry out an effective needs analysis. In order to gain a full understanding of the issue of bullying and violence in your school this chapter outlines what information you will require, what methods are available for collecting such information, and why review and evaluation are important. In keeping with the United Nations *Convention on the Rights of the Child* (1989), the chapter recommends that opportunity should be given to young people to actively involve them in the needs analysis process. The activities will enable you to develop a working group contract, generate issues, topics and questions for your needs analysis, and encourage you to think critically about the application of different methods for collecting information.

Chapter 6 Children Helping Children through Peer Support

In this chapter we consider strategies for developing peer support in school. The chapter offers a range of approaches for developing the necessary skills to set up a peer support system including:

- training peer supporters in a range of skills: active listening, attending to the other person, developing empathy, paraphrasing what the other says, offering and receiving constructive criticism;
- identifying the personal qualities of the peer supporter;
- making use of the debriefing process.

Chapter 7 Emotional Literacy in Schools

In this chapter we focus on the importance of developing emotional literacy, both at the individual as well as the organizational level. We discuss the benefits of an emotionally literate school, and illustrate with a real-life case study example derived from the Second Step Programme. The activities in this chapter focus on identifying emotions, understanding feelings and communicating empathy, and giving and receiving positive affirmation.

Chapter 8 Restorative Practice

This chapter focuses on the principles, ideas and values of restorative practice in schools and aims to familiarize readers with contemporary restorative practice applications in the school setting. Exercises and activities offer preparation for the promotion of a restorative climate in schools. A range of strategies are considered for the application of a restorative practice model in school, including a restorative response to violence, wrongdoing and everyday school problems. In this chapter we promote the idea that individuals have the potential to resolve many of their own problems. Key skills focused on in this chapter include:

- familiarization of restorative practice principles, ideas and values;
- raising awareness of contemporary restorative practice applications in the school setting;
- promoting a restorative climate in schools;
- consideration of the strategies for the application of restorative practice models in your school.

Chapter 9 The Support Group Method

This chapter focuses on the support method in which a group of peers who have been involved in a bullying incident, are guided by an adult to explore what happened and collectively to identify ways in which they can address the problem. This method adopts a problem-solving approach and makes constructive use of group processes to offer support to children who are being bullied or socially excluded by their peers.

Chapter 10 Whole-school Community Needs Analysis Checklist

In this final chapter we offer an evaluation checklist for you to use as a quick guide to monitor progress and to identify areas where you need to place more emphasis. In addition, we offer the School Climate Checklists (primary and secondary versions) for use with children and young people.

Further Reading

Cowie, H., Boardman, C., Dawkins, J. and Jennifer, D. (2004) *Emotional Health and Well-being: A Practical Guide for Schools*. London: Sage Publications.

Lee, C. (2004) *Preventing bullying in schools*. London: Paul Chapman Publishing.

Oswald, K., Safran, S. and Johanson, G. (2005) 'Preventing trouble: making schools safer places using positive behavior supports', *Education and Treatment of Children*, 28(3): 265–79.

Rivers, I. and Cowie, H. (2006) 'Bullying and homophobia at UK schools: a perspective on factors affecting resilience and recovery', *Journal of Gay and Lesbian Issues in Education*, 3(4): 11–43.

United Nations Children's Fund (UNICEF) (2007) *Child Poverty in Perspective: an Overview of Child Well-being in Rich Countries*. Innocenti Report Card 7. UNICEF Innocenti Research Centre, Florence.

World Health Organization (2002) *World Report on Violence and Health*. Geneva: World Health Organization.

Websites

Aynsley-Green, A. (2006) 'Bullying today', Office of the Children's Commissioner, www.childrenscommissioner.org/

'Bullying in schools and what to do about it' (Dr Ken Rigby's pages), www.education.unisa.edu.au/bullying

Cyberbullying, www.cyberbullying.ca and www.stopcyberbullying.org

David Knight, www.cyberbullying.info/bookcase/shelf1/knight/knight.htm

Smallwood Publishing, 'Being yourself' www.smallwood.co.uk

UK Observatory for the Promotion of Non-Violence, www.ukobservatory.com

Violence in Schools Training Action (VISTA), www.vista-europe.org

Young Women's Christian Association (YWCA) (2004) 'Pride not prejudice: young lesbian and bisexual women', YWCA Briefing, www.ywca-gb.org.uk/briefings.asp

Resources

Cowie, H. and Jennifer, D., et al. (2007) *School Bullying and Violence: Taking Action.* Guildford. European Institute of Health and Medical Sciences, University of Surrey, www.vista-europe.org

O'Moore, A.M. and Minton, S.J. (2004) *Dealing with Bullying in Schools: A Training Manual for Teachers, Parents and Other Professionals.* London: Paul Chapman Publishing.

Shariff, S. (2005) 'Cyber-dilemmas in the new millennium: balancing free expression and student safety in cyber-space', special issue: Schools and Courts: Competing Rights in the New Millennium, *McGill Journal of Education*, 40(3): 467–87.

2 | Understanding school violence

Objectives

- To help participants become aware of a multiplicity of definitions of school violence from a range of perspectives.
- To consider how a variety of factors might contribute to the development of school violence.

Introduction

Violence has been a commonplace feature of school life for centuries, with its causes embedded in the social, cultural, historical and economic contexts of the period. Those at the receiving end of violence can be individuals, objects or schools themselves, and the nature of the damage might be psychological, physical or material. Since the middle of the twentieth century, however, violence against children has increasingly been viewed as a violation of their fundamental human rights, especially their right to physical safety and psychological security and well-being. There has also been a growing concern to understand the roots of violence and to find constructive ways to reduce it and, if possible, to prevent it. The World Health Organization's (WHO, 2002) report on violence and health recommended four key steps in the process of reducing and preventing violence:

1 gathering as much knowledge as possible about the phenomenon at local, national and international levels;
2 investigating why violence occurs;
3 exploring ways to prevent violence by designing, implementing, monitoring and evaluating interventions;
4 implementing promising interventions in a range of settings, determining the cost-effectiveness of these interventions and then widely disseminating information about them.

In 1995, the Gulbenkian Foundation published a report suggesting that schools could either help prevent violence against children, or they could create an environment that reinforced violent attitudes. The report suggested that to commit to non-violence and work towards a non-violent society, schools should teach children and young people pro-social values and behaviour, discipline children and young people in a positive manner and teach children and young people non-violent conflict resolution. In adopting the whole-school community approach advocated in this book, not only will schools be able to demonstrate their commitment to non-violence as recommended by the Gulbenkian Foundation, they will also be able to meet the above four WHO recommendations.

The Nature of School Violence

Issues of Definition

This book takes the view that there is no single clear definition of violence. Instead, we think that the meaning will vary according to the individuals, communities and cultures concerned. Indeed, there is a greater awareness of the need to accept a multiplicity of definitions of school violence. These definitions will come from a range of perspectives, including those of children and young people. In taking a look at current definitions of school violence and violent behaviour, we first consider Olweus. He defined violence and violent behaviour to be 'aggressive behavior where the actor or perpetrator uses his or her own body or an object (including a weapon) to inflict (relatively serious) injury or discomfort upon another individual' (1999: 12). While this definition implies the use of physical force or power, it does not include the notion of psychological harm. The WHO defines violence as the 'intentional use of physical force or power, threatened or actual, against oneself, another person, or against a group or community, that either results in or has a high likelihood of resulting in injury, death, psychological harm, mal-development or deprivation' (2002: 5). This second definition includes the idea of intentionality and the use of power, and covers a broad range of outcomes that include psychological and physical harm. There has been little research into children and young people's definitions of school violence, although there has been some research into definitions of bullying, which is considered a subset of violent behaviour, that involves repetition over time and an imbalance of power. These studies have found that children's views of what constitutes bullying do not always match with adults' views. In fact, younger children's definitions do not necessarily match with those of older children. This shows that we all need to be aware that there are multiple definitions and that it is important for all groups within the whole-school community to understand school violence using a range of different perspectives (see Activity 2.1, p.17).

Incidence

It is difficult to be certain about the incidence of school violence, as there is a general lack of systematically collected data. Statistics from other sources give us some indication of the extent of the problem. These sources include surveys of school bullying, data on school exclusions, official statistics on accidents caused by violence, and criminal statistics based on 'legal' definitions such as antisocial behaviour, juvenile delinquency, and vandalism. Recent surveys conducted in the United Kingdom (UK) show us that:

- half of the primary school children surveyed and more than one-quarter of secondary school children reported that they had been bullied during the previous term (Oliver and Candappa, 2003);
- 10 per cent of Year 7 boys admitted carrying a knife or other weapon to school or in their neighbourhood during the preceding year. This figure rose to 24 per cent for Year 11 boys (Beinart et al., 2002);
- in one survey, 22 per cent of respondents said that they had seen a pupil attack a teacher at some point during the preceding 12 months (Beinart et al., 2002);
- 15 per cent of secondary school pupils said that they had received nasty or threatening emails or text messages during the past term (Noret and Rivers, 2006);
- the 2005 Offending, Crime and Justice Survey (Wilson et al., 2006) revealed that the majority of victimization incidents against 10- to 15-year-olds happened at school. Eleven per cent of those surveyed reported an assault without injury and 9 per cent reported personal thefts.

Context

In this book, we consider school violence to be the result of multiple levels of influence on behaviour, which include individual, relationship, social, cultural and environmental factors. We adopt an understanding of school violence that comes from the perspective of four interrelated contexts: the individual context, the interpersonal context, the community context and the context of the wider society. This idea is illustrated in Figure 2.1 and is based on a WHO model of how to understand the nature of violence.

The first of the four contexts is the *individual* context, which considers how the personal history and biological characteristics of an individual might contribute to the development of violent behaviour. For example, some children are temperamentally impulsive, they may find it hard to manage their feelings

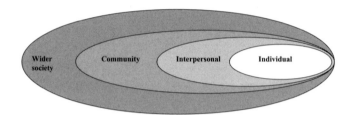

Figure 2.1 Model for understanding the nature of school violence (reproduced by kind permission of WHO Press)

Source: adapted from WHO, 2002: 12, fig. 1.3.

and they may have a low tolerance for frustration. At the individual level, addressing violence involves consideration of the individual risk factors listed in Table 2.1 and taking steps to modify individual risk behaviours through, for example, the Support Group Method (outlined in Chapter 9).

Table 2.1 Risk factors for youth crime

Individual
Impulsiveness, hyperactivity, restlessness and limited concentration span
Low intelligence and poor performance at school, aggressive behaviour at school, lack of commitment to school including truancy
Alienation from the mainstream and lack of social commitment
Attitudes that condone problem behaviour (drug abuse, youth crime, school-age pregnancy, school failure)
Early involvement in problem behaviour

Interpersonal
Harsh or erratic parental supervision and discipline, cold or rejecting parental attitudes, physical abuse
Family conflict, parental separation, family history of problem behaviour such as drug or alcohol addiction and criminal activity, parental involvement in drug abuse or crime, parental attitudes condoning problem behaviour
Large family and young parents
Social and economic deprivation, low family income and poor housing
Friends involved in problem behaviour

Community
Disorganized inner-city areas, characterized by physical deterioration and neglect, overcrowded households, publicly subsidized rented accommodation, high residential mobility, high turnover of residents and lack of neighbourhood attachment
School disorganization including low staff morale, poor classroom management, frequent pupil punishment, lack of praise for pupils and weak leadership from head teachers and governors
Presence of gangs, weapons and drugs
Lack of social capital

Wider society
Economic and social inequalities between different groups
Political structures such as the extent to which a society enforces its existing laws on violence and social protection by the state
Cultural influences such as violence endorsed as a normal method to resolve conflicts and the teaching of norms and values that support violent behaviour

Source: Beinart et al. (2002); Farrington (1996); WHO (2002)

The second level, the *interpersonal* context, considers the manner in which adults and young people communicate, both at home and at school. It also considers how these interactions may then lead to the development of particular behaviour patterns. For example, the socialization that a young person experiences with adults and with peers may help to develop healthy and effective strategies to cope with violence. On the other hand, a young person may be drawn into relationships with aggressive peers and adults who provide mutual support and possibly active encouragement for acting aggressively. At the interpersonal level, addressing school violence involves placing a strong emphasis on the development of pro-social relationships, emotional literacy and effective communication (see Chapters 6 and 7 for more detail on strategies that help to achieve this).

The third level of the model focuses on the *community* context in which interpersonal relationships occur, which is in this case schools and neighbourhoods. At this level, the model will help to identify those settings that are associated with an increased risk of violent behaviour. Risk factors at this level may include high levels of residential mobility, heterogeneity, high population density, high levels of unemployment, and local drug-dealing activity. For example, specific characteristics of a neighbourhood, such as violent behaviour, weapon-carrying and gang feuds on the streets, can permeate into school communities and support violent attitudes and behaviours. Addressing school violence at this level emphasizes the need to resolve conflict through dialogue or other non-violent means to help strengthen healthy interpersonal relationships within the whole-school community. This can be achieved through the development of a conflict resolution and mediation programme, such as the ones described in Chapter 8.

The focus of the final context relates to factors in the *wider society* that can influence engagement in violent behaviour. These factors include the prevailing social and cultural norms and values that might support violence as an acceptable way of resolving conflict. Such factors might include the placing of adult rights over child welfare, male dominance over women and children, the use of excessive force by police against citizens, and norms that support political conflict. Take, for example, the stereotypical male attitudes and behaviours such as competition, physical aggression, overt racism and homophobia, open peer criticism and a lack of emotional skills. These attitudes and behaviours can idealize what it is to be masculine (for example, 'boys will be boys'). Such attitudes can reinforce, both directly and indirectly, attitudes and practices within schools. If we use the 'boys will be boys' example, staff and other pupils may be unwilling to intervene in a physical conflict between two boys. This may also result in a general lack of support for children and young people who are experiencing problems (Carter, 2002).

The wider society context includes other factors, such as the health, educational, economic and social policies that maintain high levels of economic or social inequality between groups in society. For example, people in capitalist societies tend to behave in an individualistic, competitive manner. This perpetuates differences in social class and worsens the plight of disadvantaged groups. Recent surveys have shown how communities with a strong commitment to equality of opportunity, voluntary cooperation and high moral discipline exhibit lower levels of aggressive behaviour (Bergeron and Schneider, 2005). This book takes the view that in order to address school violence at this level, it is important to promote values of cooperation, collaboration and partnership. This can be achieved through actively encouraging all members of the whole-school community to work together to develop a positive and supportive culture within which to work and learn. Chapter 8 considers restorative practice as one way of achieving this.

It almost goes without saying that the absence of such risk factors will help protect children and young people against involvement in crime, drug abuse and antisocial behaviour. There are a number of other protective factors that may help to protect children and young people from offending, especially those from high-risk backgrounds. Farrington (1996) suggests that understanding and building upon these protective factors, which are summarized in Table 2.2, will increase the effectiveness of violence-prevention strategies.

Table 2.2 Protective factors for youth crime

Individual characteristics
Female gender
Resilient temperament
A sense of self-efficacy
A positive, outgoing disposition
High intelligence
Interpersonal
A strong sense of attachment to one or both parents, characterized by a stable, warm and affectionate relationship
Parents who maintain a strong interest in their children's education
Opportunities for consultation, shared social activities and positive involvement in family and school life
Parents and teachers who provide effective supervision, clear rules and consistent discipline
Parents, teachers and peers who hold pro-social attitudes and model positive social behaviour
Recognition and due praise within the family and the school
Community
Opportunities to feel positively involved in the life of the school and the local community
Parents, teachers and community leaders who lead by example and hold clearly stated expectations regarding behaviour
Encouragement for all children and young people to fulfil their potential
Wider society
Healthy social attitudes towards antisocial and criminal behaviour

Source: Beinart et al. (2002); Farrington (1996); Youth Justice Board (2005)

Activities for the Training Event

Activity 2.1 Defining School Violence (90 minutes)

Purpose
- To give participants the opportunity to develop their own definition of school violence.
- To demonstrate that a range of perspectives are equally valid without any one definition necessarily being 'right or wrong'.
- To encourage the skills of listening, peaceful negotiation, collaboration and cooperation.

Materials
Small index cards and pens.

Procedure
1 Divide the group into subgroups of four participants each. Ask the groups to appoint a scribe who will not participate, but record ideas. Ask the group to brainstorm a list of ideas regarding the nature of school violence for about 10 minutes (each group will need at least nine ideas). Ask the scribe to write each idea on one card, that is, one idea/suggestion per card. Discourage group discussion or judgement at this stage. Prompt questions might include:
   (a) *What types of violent behaviours are we talking about?*
   (b) *Who or what are we talking about?*
   (c) *How is the violent behaviour inflicted?*
   (d) *What is the nature of the damage caused by school violence?*
   (e) *What consequences are suffered and by whom/what?*

2 The aim of the second part of this activity is to help participants discuss the relative importance of different aspects of school violence and develop a definition. Ask each subgroup to remove any duplicate cards and to select nine cards to rank in order of priority. Ask each group to arrange the cards in a diamond pattern with the most valued item at the top and the least valued at the bottom (see Figure 2.2). Each group can decide upon the criteria for selection, which might include, for example, *'the most or least important'* or the *'most relevant'*. Encourage participants within their subgroups to discuss their decisions. If the subgroups are able to reach consensus (and they might not, which is fine!), ask them to write down their definition of school violence on a card based on the outcome of the activity.

Discussion
This activity will probably result in animated discussion! Point out that this activity enables participants to become aware of the multiplicity of definitions of school violence. With the whole group, focus the discussion upon how the

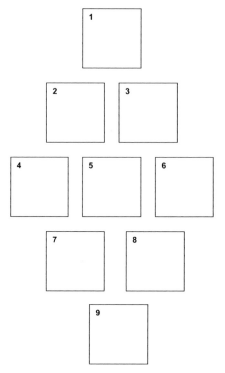

Figure 2.2 Diamond ranking

subgroups arrived at decisions during the ranking activity and how/if they reached consensus. What are the similarities and differences between the subgroup definitions? Further prompt questions might include the following:

- *What are the implications of different groups within your whole-school community holding different definitions of school violence?*
- *What is the relevance of this activity for your whole-school community understanding of school violence?*
- *What are the implications of these multiple definitions for preventing and reducing school violence?*

Emphasize that the point of the activity is *not* to reach a consensus on a definition for school violence. Rather, through the process of discussion and recognition of a multiplicity of definitions, the aim is to heighten awareness and deepen understanding of the phenomenon of school violence.

Activity 2.2 The Nature of School Violence (60 minutes)

Purpose
- To enable participants to identify what they know about the interrelated contexts of school violence.

Materials
Film stimulus such as *Bully Dance* (Perlman, 2000) or *Silent Witnesses* (O'Moore, 2006) (see Resources, p. 20).
Flip chart and pens.

Procedure
Show the 10-minute film to the whole group. After the film, divide the whole group into subgroups of three or four participants. In their subgroups, ask participants to consider and discuss the following:

- the individual characteristics of the protagonists involved;
- the violent events that took place;
- where the violence took place;
- the influence of the four interrelated contexts, that is, individual characteristics, interpersonal relationships, the whole-school community and wider society.

It might be helpful to replay the film, with the volume down, during the activity. Allow at least 30 minutes for this part of the activity. Ask subgroups to nominate a representative to feedback key findings to the main group. Allow five minutes for each subgroup. The facilitator should summarize on a flip chart the key points under each of the consideration points above.

Discussion
Explore common and contrasting themes that emerge from each of the group's presentations. Ask the group to consider what the implications of the contextual influences are for preventing and reducing school violence. What are the implications of different groups within your whole-school community understanding the nature of school violence from different perspectives?

Further Reading

Barak, G. (2003) *Violence and Nonviolence: Pathways to Understanding*. London: Sage Publications.

Daiute, C., Beykont, Z., Higson-Smith, C. and Nucci, L. (2006) *International Perspectives on Youth Conflict and Development*. Oxford: Oxford University Press.

Debarbieux, E. and Blaya, C. (eds) (2001) *Violence in Schools: Ten Approaches in Europe*. Issy les Moulineaux: ESF.

Debarbieux, E. and Blaya, C. (eds) (2002) *Violence in Schools and Public Policies*. Paris: Elsevier.

Hayden, C. (2007) *Children in Trouble: The Role of Families, Schools and Communities*. Basingstoke: Palgrave Macmillan.

Smith, P.K. (ed.) (2003) *Violence in Schools: The Response in Europe*. London: RoutledgeFalmer.

Websites

Cowie, H. and Jennifer, D. et al. (2007) *School Bullying and Violence: Taking Action*, www.vista-europe.org

UK Observatory for the Promotion of Non-Violence, www.ukobservatory.com

Resources

O'Moore, M. (2006) *Silent Witnesses*. Ireland: Trinity College Dublin Anti-Bullying Research and Resource Centre, www.abc.tcd.ie

Perlman, J. (2000) *Bully Dance* (*La Danse des Brutes*). Canada: National Film Board of Canada, www.bullfrogfilms.com/catalog/bully.html

3 | Working with the whole-school community

Objectives

- To understand what we mean by a whole-school community approach.
- To increase awareness of the relationships among different sections of your school community.
- To have an understanding of how to include all members of the whole-school community in the promotion of non-violence.

What Is the Whole-school Community?

Given our understanding of school violence is of multiple causes in terms of the interaction of risk factors operating among four levels (see Chapter 2), it seems appropriate to consider its prevention and reduction from a whole-school community perspective. Violence at school is not simply a school problem; specific characteristics of the local neighbourhood and wider community, such as the strong presence of racial tension, often pervade school communities, creating a climate of fear and anxiety among young people and staff that supports violent attitudes and behaviour. Any action a school takes in response to violence among their children and young people is, therefore, more likely to succeed if it involves families, services and agencies from the local community.

Thus, at the heart of a whole-school community approach is the notion that addressing school violence is a collective challenge. From this viewpoint, the whole-school community approach to addressing school violence involves all members of the school community including children and young people, school management, teaching staff, non-teaching staff, school nurses, lunchtime supervisors, parents and carers, school governors, the local community and external organizations (see Figure 3.1 for an illustration of a whole-school community approach to the promotion of non-violence).

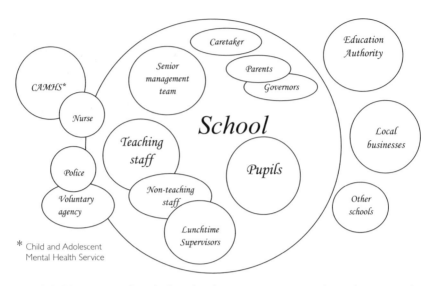

Figure 3.1 Illustration of a whole-school community approach to the promotion of non-violence. See also pages 29 and 33.

While much has been written about the importance of involving all members of the whole-school community in addressing violence, little has been written about how to put this into practice. The main aim of this chapter, therefore, is to introduce you to some practical ideas and resources that you could use to engage different members of the school community in the reduction and prevention of violence. These ideas range from involving children and young people in your needs analysis (see Chapter 4 for a definition), to engaging external agencies to form partnerships in the reduction and prevention of violence. While the suggestions presented here are not intended to be exhaustive, our aim is to provide you with examples of what is possible, based on our research, which we hope will support you to find your own solutions.

Picking a few elements of an intervention to reduce and prevent violence and introducing it as an 'add on' or as a 'quick fix' will not have the desired outcome. Similarly, involving a non-representative group to manage the project, without the involvement of the wider school community, will result in disappointment. If an intervention has any chance of succeeding it needs to involve the participation of everyone, including children and young people, teaching and non-teaching staff, parents and carers, governors and outside agencies. The success of your needs analysis and subsequent intervention will depend upon the extent to which all members of the school community feel empowered to participate meaningfully in its development and implementation. A lack of 'ownership' of the intervention will almost certainly result in resistance. Besides, involving all members of the school community enables you to draw upon a wide range of skills and expertise to help with specific tasks. For example, a head teacher recently told us at a workshop we were running that he did not have the time or financial resources to carry out a needs analysis, to which we offered a number of suggestions. We suggested that children and young people, acting as peer researchers, could carry out parts of the needs analysis (see Chapter 5) during their Citizenship lessons. We proposed the involvement of parents and carers as volunteers in the needs analysis, which would also have the added benefit of boosting their participation in school life. We recommended support from the wider community in the form of engaging a university student wishing to carry out postgraduate research.

In harmony with the United Nations *Convention on the Rights of the Child* (UN, 1989), *Every Child Matters* (DfES, 2003) and the Children Act 2004, one of the core principles of a whole-school community approach is to encompass the rights of democracy, participation and citizenship. Prepared by young people across Europe, upon the initiative of the Council of Europe, the *European Charter for Democratic Schools Without Violence* (2004; see Box 3.1) offers a fundamental set of values and principles that encompasses these rights. Intended as a document to be applied by all those involved in the life of the school, the charter might serve as a contract to be signed by all members of the school community as a sound basis for the promotion of non-violence.

Box 3.1 *European Charter for Democratic Schools Without Violence* **(2004)**

- All members of the school community have the right to a safe and peaceful school. Everyone has the responsibility to contribute to creating a positive and inspiring environment for learning and personal development.
- Everyone has the right to equal treatment and respect regardless of any personal difference. Everyone enjoys freedom of speech without risking discrimination or repression.
- The school community ensures that everybody is aware of their rights and responsibilities.
- Every democratic school has a democratically elected decision-making body composed of representatives of students, teachers, parents, and other members of the school community where appropriate. All members of this body have the right to vote.
- In a democratic school, conflicts are resolved in a non-violent and constructive way in partnership with all members of the school community. Every school has staff and pupils trained to prevent and solve conflicts through counselling and mediation.
- Every case of violence is investigated and dealt with promptly, and followed through irrespective of whether pupils or any other members of the school community are involved.
- School is a part of the local community. Co-operation and exchange of information with local partners are essential for preventing and solving problems.

Benefits of Working with the Whole-school Community

A whole-school community approach is necessary for the successful promotion of non-violence in school. Without a whole-school community
approach, your chosen intervention is unlikely to reach all children and
young people in your school or, indeed, other members of the school community. A whole-school community approach is more likely to succeed if
the school's leadership and management style is democratic, if communication and relationships among all members of the school community are
dynamic, and if goals and values are shared among all interested parties.
More specifically, the impact on children and young people in your school
will be to develop their capacity to:

• enhance their emotional health and well-being;
• participate in decisions that affect their school community;
• respect others' rights and integrity;
• value cultural diversity and develop solidarity among peers from different backgrounds;
• work cooperatively and recognize responsibilities towards others and
  society as a whole.

The impact on educators will be to develop their capacity to:

• foster dynamic relationships with children and young people, school
  staff, parents, governors and the wider community;
• enhance children and young people's participation in decision-making;
• focus on the wider curriculum and the development of an emotionally
  literate organization;
• work from a set of shared values and goals;
• participate meaningfully in decision-making and management of the
  school;
• identify and implement their own training needs;
• develop appropriate links with relevant agencies and services in the community and nationally (for example, in education, social services, police and
  justice, youth and social sectors, non-governmental organizations (NGOs)).

Some Suggestions for Involving the Whole-school Community

In order to address the promotion of non-violence in school effectively,
schools must develop flexible ways of working with professionals in education, health, and social services, and other members of the community, as
well as parents and young people themselves. We have adapted a four-level
model of involvement for a whole-school community approach to the promotion of non-violence (see Figure 3.2), originally proposed by Robson

(1996) and extended by Shaughnessy (2006). This model takes account of four interrelated levels of involvement: information, participation, collaboration and partnership. At the information level, the emphasis is on the provision of information about their promotion of non-violence work by the school to parents and the wider community. At the participation level, while involvement of the whole-school community is more extensive, participation is still essentially passive, for example, through meetings, assemblies and workshops. On the other hand, the final two levels of the model focus on all members of the school community working together to share the responsibility for the promotion of non-violence as collaborators and partners. The remainder of this chapter identifies a number of means by which the four levels of involvement are achievable.

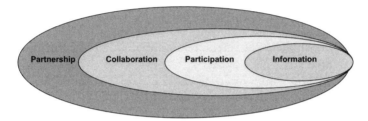

Figure 3.2 Model of involvement for a whole-school community approach to the promotion of non-violence
Source: adapted from Robson, 1996.

Levels of Involvement

Information

Generate 'Welcome' letters to all new pupils and their parents/carers to the school.

Circulate a promotion of non-violence newsletter two or three times a year to families, relevant agencies and services in the local community highlighting areas of concern, intervention plans, updates on progress, strategies for children and young people to address violence, information about school and community resources, links to Internet resources.

Hold evening meetings to inform parents/carers and members of the local community about the issue of violence in your school, your needs analysis and intervention plans, and regular assemblies to keep children and young people and staff up to date.

Introduce parent and staff resource packs to include information about types of violence, causes, effects, strategies for helping children and young people address violence, reading lists of children's literature dealing with the topic of bullying and violence (see www.anti-bullying alliance.org.uk/downloads/pdf/draftbullyingbooksforchildrenandyoung people210606.pdf.

Distribute information leaflets about your project to houses in the immediate neighbourhood.

Use magazines, newsletters, leaflets, and websites available from voluntary agencies (for example, ChildLine, the National Children's Bureau (NCB), the National Society for the Prevention of Cruelty to Children (NSPCC) and YoungMinds) to provide information about bullying and violence in school.

Participation

Involve members of the parent–teacher association in your efforts to promote non-violence, perhaps as representatives in your needs analysis working group (see Chapter 5).

Extend training in the promotion of non-violence to parents/carers, non-teaching staff (including school nurses, school counsellors, lunchtime supervisors, school bus drivers and caretakers) and governors.

Organize assemblies that celebrate days that are linked to global citizenship (see Box 3.2).

Engage a theatre company to deliver a professional performance related to the promotion of non-violence to children and young people, school staff and parents/carers (for example, Actionwork).

Invite ChildLine in Partnership with Schools (CHIPS) to deliver a workshop or seminar on bullying and peer support.

Invite your local Police Community Support Officer (PCSO) to deliver wider crime reduction education through Citizenship lessons, and after school and lunchtime activities (see Case Study 3.1, p. 28).

Box 3.2 An assembly calendar (adapted from Shaughnessy, 2006)

One of the ways to demonstrate your commitment to the prevention and reduction of school violence is to organize a series of assemblies for all members of the whole-school community to celebrate days that are linked to global citizenship. These will help to raise awareness of issues such as empathy for others, a sense of identity, value and respect for diversity, a concern for social justice and equity, and a concern for the environment. Religious festivals are intentionally not included.

Month	Topic	Suggestions
January	Holocaust memorial day	Use literature such as *The Diary of Anne Frank* as an introduction to the issues
February	Social justice day	Discuss the reasons for, and the consequences of, the Holocaust Focus on people who have worked for equity in their lifetimes (for example, Mother Theresa, the Dalai Lama, Nelson Mandela)

continued opposite

Box 3.2 continued

Month	Topic	Suggestions
March	World book day	Share stories from different cultures and traditions
April	Disability awareness day	Celebrate the achievements of a famous disabled person Raise issues of disability with the pupils
May	Self-esteem day	Celebrate the achievements and talents of parents, pupils and staff in the school
June	World environment day	Investigate a local or global environmental issue
July	Creativity day	Draw on a range of traditions to celebrate the visual and performing arts
September	Sustainable development day	Focus on sustainable lifestyles, reducing waste and taking care of the environment
October	Black history month	Celebrate Black history
November	International children's day	Focus on the rights of children
December	Human rights day	Discuss the human rights legislation and its meaning for pupils and staff

© Council of Europe

Collaboration

Involve lunchtime supervisors in engaging children in structured activities, such as ball games, skipping games, gym activities during the lunch hour.

Encourage local media coverage of the school's efforts to promote non-violence.

Invite children and young people and staff to write poems about violence in school as a means of raising awareness of the issue and involve the local newspaper in publishing them.

Meet with community leaders to discuss the school's promotion of non-violence plans.

Provide opportunities for children and young people to discuss the school's plans with members of the local community.

Engage the wider community in your efforts to promote non-violence, for example, through presentations, or the introduction of elements of your intervention, to out-of-school activities such as Sunday schools, youth clubs, Brownies or Cubs.

Develop links with other schools in your area to share your experiences regarding the promotion of non-violence.

Invite parents/carers to help with your needs analysis tasks, such as photocopying questionnaires and data collection.

Engage the school nurse to help with data collection for your needs analysis.

Set up a peer support system (see Chapter 6).

Partnership

Invite a known personality or celebrity to act as a patron for your project.

Integrate the local police into your plans through the Safer Schools Partnerships programme, which offers a local multi-agency partnership approach to crime prevention, school safety, behaviour improvement and educational achievement (see Case Study 3.1).

Develop a partnership with your local Child and Adolescent Mental Health Service (CAMHS). For example, in Surrey, the local CAMHS works closely with school staff and young people to set up, train, support, and develop peer support services in school.

Take part in Anti-Bullying Week at regional or national level, an initiative coordinated by the Anti-Bullying Alliance (ABA). Working closely with the National Healthy Schools Programme, the Secondary and Primary National Strategies, the ABA delivers a programme of national and regional support.

Encourage your children and young people to get involved with Child-Line by joining a ChildLine Advisory Team to help shape the services that ChildLine provides or by seeking work experience.

Engage the services of a national agency that provides specialist training, such as Leap Confronting Conflict or Antidote, to audit, develop and manage your intervention, and integrate it as part of your School Development Plan (see Case Study 3.2).

Invite local businesses to support the work of your school through sponsorship.

Get involved with your local Healthy Schools Scheme.

Put a restorative philosophy into practice (see Chapter 8).

Case Study 3.1 Working with the local police

This girls' secondary school in south-west London was experiencing antisocial behaviour outside the school gates and thefts inside the school premises. The Safer Neighbourhoods team, a Metropolitan Police initiative, worked with young people and staff to address the problem. One of the PCSOs took responsibility for overseeing the partnership. His tasks included; organizing external patrols to reduce antisocial behaviour and parking problems at the end of the school day; internal patrols to help young people get to know the local police; meetings with young people, parents and teachers to discuss crime issues; and talks with young people about bullying and harassment. The school management team supplied information to the Safer Neighbourhoods team, enabling them to make arrests for theft. Within six months, not only had antisocial behaviour

continued opposite

Case Study 3.1 continued

around the school been greatly reduced, young people were much happier talking to local police officers both within and outside school. The positive relationship that the Safer Neighbourhoods team has developed with this school continues: future plans include talks about crime-related issues, greater involvement of teachers in police dealings with young people and a continued regular police presence in and around the school premises.

Case Study 3.2 Working with a national voluntary organization

(adapted from Cowie et al., 2004)

A large mixed comprehensive school in the heart of London's East End was experiencing high levels of violence and conflict, heightened by racial tension, which had spilled over from the local community. The head teacher approached a national voluntary youth organization, Leap Confronting Conflict, to support the school in developing a programme to address the issue. Following an initial conflict audit, a programme was tailor-made for the school, which included training for children and young people, an intensive residential weekend for selected young people and staff, a peer training programme for older pupils to work with younger ones, youth mediation training and staff training sessions. Benefits of participating in the programme included a positive change in school culture and ethos, a reduction in high-level conflict with bullying less likely to escalate into physical violence, staff confidence to deal with conflicts when they did occur, and increased student self-esteem, self-confidence and responsibility.

Activities for the Training Event

Activity 3.1 Understanding Your School's Level of Involvement (60 minutes)

Purpose
- To increase awareness of the relationships among different sections of your school community.
- To understand the distribution of partnerships within the school community.
- To generate discussion about how to fill the gaps and increase the levels of involvement of other members of the whole-school community.

Materials
    Pens and paper.
    Activity Handout 3.1, p. 33.

Procedure
Divide participants into subgroups to produce Euler circles of your school's levels of involvement. Describe the process of Euler (pronounced Oiler)

circles (see Activity Handout 3.1 for examples). Swiss-born mathematician and physicist Leonhard Euler (1707–83) invented Euler circles, a diagrammatic method for visualizing information that represents partnerships, exclusions and intersections of different groups (similar to the more commonly known Venn diagram). This method of visualization provides a powerful means of graphically illustrating your school's current relationships and partnerships. The drawing consists of two or more circles, each representing a different group, partner, agency, programme, and so on. Overlapping circles represent a shared relationship, or partnership; the degree to which the circles overlap represents the strength of the relationship or partnership; and the size of the circles are relative to the groups' importance. Circles are contained within a circle if they are part of the larger circle's organization so, for example, the circle that represents your pupils would be contained with the larger circle representing your school. Ask subgroups to create an Euler circle of your school's relationships and partnerships. After about 40 minutes, ask the groups to present their Euler circles to the main group.

Discussion

Analyse key similarities and differences between the subgroups' diagrams and the underlying reasons for these. Following analysis of all of the Euler circles, participants can discuss ways of filling partnership gaps and encouraging links with the wider community. Some prompt questions for discussion might include:

- *What do the diagrams tell us about the school's current levels of involvement of the whole-school community?*
- *How would participants like to see the levels of involvement change?*
- *What problems do you envisage by involving other members of the whole-school community?*
- *What benefits do you anticipate by involving other members of the whole-school community?*

Activity 3.2 Enhancing your School's Partnerships (90 minutes)

Purpose
- To encourage participants to think creatively about different sections of the whole-school community and how they might be involved in their school's promotion of non-violence venture.
- To enhance group dynamics.

Materials
   Flip chart paper and pens.

Procedure
Divide participants into small groups of three to four participants accord-

ing to their role (that is, pupils, teaching staff, parents, and so on). Ask the subgroups to brainstorm a list of issues, topics and questions that they would like to see addressed in their school's reduction and prevention of violence plans. Encourage the subgroups to think widely. Encourage quantity rather than quality: the more ideas the better. Ask a scribe from each group to write down the ideas in the order that they are generated on a piece of flip chart paper entitled 'Issues, Topics, Questions'. When the subgroups have each generated a list, ask them to brainstorm a second list of reasons why the issues, topics and questions generated in the first list might be difficult to achieve. For example, it might be difficult to carry out a needs analysis prior to implementing an intervention due to financial constraints. Ask a scribe from each group to write down the ideas in the order that they are generated on a second piece of flip chart paper entitled 'Difficulties'. Finally, ask groups to brainstorm how different members from the whole-school community might be able to resolve the difficulties generated in the second list to achieve the issues, topics and questions generated in the first list. For example, if a school requires financial support to carry out a needs analysis, they might consider asking the parent–teacher association to help with fund-raising from local businesses. Ask a scribe from each group to write down the ideas in the order that they are generated on a third piece of flip chart paper entitled 'Whole-School Community Solutions'.

Discussion

Ask each group to present three of their issues, and corresponding difficulties and whole-school community solutions to the main group. Encourage participants to add to and share ideas. After exposing participants to a wide range of solutions, they can think about how to use them in real-life situations. It is a good time to get participants to reflect upon the rich variety of solutions available and to realize that a variety of solutions are at hand to address each issue, topic and question. The point can also be made that by collectively addressing the promotion of non-violence, schools can draw upon a broader range of expertise and experience of other members and organizations from within the whole-school community, than if they try to go it alone.

Further Reading

Gittins, C. (ed.) (2006) *Violence Reduction in Schools – How to Make a Difference*. Strasbourg: Council of Europe Publishing.

O'Moore, M. and Minton, S. (2004) *Dealing with Bullying in Schools: A Training Manual for Teachers, Parents and Other Professionals*. London: Paul Chapman Publishing.

Sharp, S. and Smith, P.K. (eds) (1994) *Tackling Bullying in Your School*. London: Routledge.

Smith, P.K. and Sharp, S. (eds) (1994) *School Bullying: Insights and Perspectives*. London: Routledge.

Websites

Actionwork, www.actionwork.com
Antidote, www.antidote.org.uk
Anti-Bullying Alliance, www.anti-bullyingalliance.org.uk
ChildLine in Partnership with Schools, www.childline.org.uk
Cowie, H. and Jennifer, D. et al. (2007) *School Bullying and Violence: Taking Action*. http://www.vista-europe.org
Don't Suffer in Silence, www.dfes.gov.uk/bullying
Health Promoting Schools Scheme
    http://healthpromotingschools.co.uk/index.asp
Healthy Schools Scheme, www.healthyschools.gov.uk
Leap Confronting Conflict, www.leaplinx.com
National Children's Bureau, www.ncb.org.uk
National Society for the Prevention of Cruelty to Children, www.nspcc.org.uk
Safer School Partnerships, www.everychildmatters.gov.uk/ete/ssp/
UK Observatory for the Promotion of Non-Violence
    http://www.ukobservatory.com
YoungMinds, www.youngminds.org.uk

Resources

Department for Education and Employment (1999) *National Healthy School Standard Guidance*. Nottingham: Author.
Department for Education and Employment (2001) *National Healthy School Standard Getting Started – A Guide for Schools*. Nottingham: Department for Education and Skills.
Erceg, E. and Cross, D. (2004) *Friendly Schools and Families*. Camberwell, Australia. Australian Council for Educational Research Press. http://www.friendlyschools.com.au.

Activity Handout 3.1 Euler circles

In the fictitious example below, participants from School A have produced a very different diagram to participants from School B. School A have mapped a wide range of groups who have collaborative relationships and active partnerships with the school. This school could be said to be demonstrating a whole-school community approach to the promotion of non-violence. School B has less active involvement with interested groups within the school and none without. This school could be said to be involving the whole-school community at minimal levels.

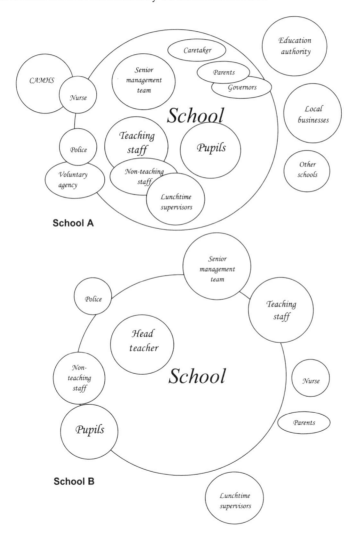

Preparing for change

Objectives

- To recognize the notion of a school's *readiness* for change.
- To promote a clear understanding of what we mean by a needs analysis.
- To encourage readers to develop a working group to oversee the needs analysis.

What Is a Needs Analysis?

Needs analysis describes a range of activities and processes that provide a school with a structured and impartial means of identifying the needs of a specific group, assessing the availability of resources to meet those needs, and planning and selecting an appropriate intervention or set of interventions. Also known as a self-audit or self-evaluation, a needs analysis is an essential prerequisite for effectively implementing an intervention for the promotion and reduction of school violence.

A needs analysis involves eight steps: (1) collecting information about the school setting and people; (2) identifying the bullying and violence issues; (3) designing a set of shared goals; (4) identifying available resources; (5) identifying potential difficulties; (6) planning the intervention; (7) promoting the intervention; and (8) monitoring and evaluating the intervention (see Figure 4.1).

Step 1 Collecting Information on the Setting and the People

- What is the vision of the head teacher?
- What is the culture of the school?
- What is the ethos/philosophy of the school?
- How well does practice match philosophy in the school?
- Who makes decisions in the school and how?

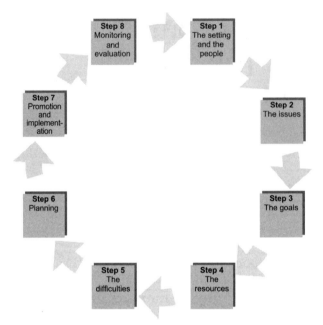

Figure 4.1 Carrying out a needs analysis
Source: adapted from Cowie et al. 2004

Step 2 Identifying the Issues

- What is the nature of the bullying and violence problems experienced by young people in the school?
- How do you know that these are problems faced by young people in your school?
- What problems do you intend to address?
- Why have you selected these specific problems to address?
- What positive anti-bullying and behaviour management policies and practices are currently in place in your school?
- Where do you need to take further action?

Step 3 Designing a Set of Shared Goals

- What changes do you want to see?
- Do your colleagues, young people and parents share your goals?

Step 4 Identifying the Resources

- What are the financial resources available?
- What are the material resources available?
- What are the human and organizational resources available?
- What are the particular strengths of your school, colleagues and young

people in relation to the changes you plan to make?

- Can you do anything to increase or make better use of these resources?

Step 5 Identifying Potential Difficulties

- What might get in the way of achieving your goals?
- What can you do from the outset to prevent these potential difficulties from becoming actual difficulties?
- Can you change these difficulties into change facilitators?

Step 6 Planning the Intervention

- What are the possible interventions available?
- Have these interventions been evaluated? If so, what are the advantages and disadvantages of each?
- Is a particular intervention suitable for the goals and issues outlined in Steps 2 and 3?
- Does your chosen intervention need tailoring to suit the needs analysis?

Step 7 Promoting and Implementing the Intervention

- Decide on a launch date.
- Devise publicity materials, for example, posters, badges, leaflets, notice-boards.
- Use the materials to publicize the intervention as widely as possible, both within school and outside school.
- Invite a known local personality or celebrity to be a 'moral sponsor' or patron for the intervention.
- Invite representatives from local shops, businesses and newspapers to a presentation of the intervention in order to gather both general and possibly financial support.
- Nominate young people to be ambassadors for the intervention.

Step 8 Monitoring and Evaluation

- Do you have ways to evaluate whether you are achieving your goals?
- Do you have ways of measuring unexpected changes/developments?
- What will you do if your evaluation does not produce the results you had hoped to achieve?

Benefits of a Needs Analysis

We consider there are a number of benefits to conducting a needs analysis, which include the following:

- the opportunity to raise awareness of the issue of bullying and violence in your school among all members of the school community, including pupils, staff and parents, and motivating individuals to take action;
- the opportunity to ascertain the nature and extent of bullying and violence in your school;
- the provision of information upon which you can base your decision about which intervention, or range of interventions, is most suited to your situation;
- the opportunity to establish a baseline measure against which to track and evaluate the effectiveness of your chosen intervention(s);
- the opportunity to involve representatives from all areas of the school community, a key starting point towards effective implementation of an intervention;
- the opportunity for all members of the school community to work co-operatively towards a common goal.

Despite the advantages of carrying out a needs analysis, there are several difficulties with the process (Cowie and Wallace, 2000). One common difficulty is the issue of encouraging individuals or particular groups of individuals to respond to requests for involvement, for example, to attend a meeting or to complete a questionnaire. Another problem is the collection of conflicting information. For example, in some schools a large percentage of pupils may indicate the presence of high levels of bullying while the staff or board of governors may deny its existence. The most challenging situation for anyone involved in carrying out a needs analysis is when they discover that the findings contradict their personal beliefs or views. In addition, the process of conducting a needs analysis can be very resource-consuming in terms of financial, human and time resources.

Nevertheless, if interventions to reduce bullying and violence are to be successful, they need to be systematically planned, implemented and evaluated. Interventions are more likely to work if they are based on a full understanding of the issues, knowledge of the resources available, and an awareness of the potential difficulties that may arise in the course of planning and implementing the intervention. A needs analysis provides one means of achieving this. However, conducting a needs analysis is rarely a 'one-off' procedure; rather, it presents an ongoing and demanding process. Furthermore, instituting change requires a transition to new ways of working that can be challenging and, at times, disturbing (Cowie and Wallace, 2000). This can be aided by an attempt on the part of the senior management team to understand the process of change that is taking place, to work collaboratively over time with the other key stakeholders involved, and to develop the stance of reflective evaluation from a range of perspectives (Cowie et al., 2004).

The Process of Change

A range of organizational factors can either support or impede the process of change. Of particular relevance are how the school operates as an organization, the quality of leadership and the quality of the school culture. At the organizational level, a school is more likely to have success in adopting and sustaining an intervention when all members of the school community share the same values, are involved in decision-making processes, and are willing and able to act within a consistent framework (Roffey, 2000). Good leadership can be identified as a clear vision of the head teacher counterbalanced with the active involvement of staff and pupils in decision-making and developing a 'shared ethos' (Sammons et al., 1995). A strong culture is a significant determinant of both effectiveness and change and is characterized by a commitment to a set of values held by most staff, loyalty to organizational goals, and a mutual support system (Robbins, 1994). A school's readiness to change, therefore, will be dependent upon the extent to which elements of these factors support the introduction of a needs analysis, and whether all members of the school community are empowered to participate meaningfully in its development.

Is Your School Ready to Conduct a Needs Analysis?

It is essential that the process of conducting a needs analysis is one of participation involving all members of the whole-school community at each stage. Research has identified two key conditions relating to the implementation of a successful needs analysis (Meuret and Morlaix, 2003). The first condition relates to the importance of the composition of the working group in the early stages of the needs analysis (also known as the steering group) (see Chapter 5) and its ability to motivate different members of the whole-school community. The second relates to the means by which the initial stages of the needs analysis are conducted in order to establish which issues require further investigation. The participation of all members of the whole-school community in the process of conducting a needs analysis is important for two reasons. First, if the process of engaging in a needs analysis is grounded in discussions with all members of the whole-school community, it is more likely that interpersonal relationships will improve among them. Second, involvement in the process of self-evaluation enhances individual commitment to the project and a sense of 'ownership'. Furthermore, results of research conducted recently in the UK suggest that a school's readiness and ability to carry out a needs analysis are important prerequisites for the successful implementation of an intervention to promote non-violence (see Case Study 4.1).

Case Study 4.1 *Readiness* **to conduct a needs analysis**
(Jennifer and Shaughnessy, 2005)

A longitudinal study was carried out over one academic year with seven study schools, one of the main aims of which was to explore the introduction and integration of *Checkpoints* (Varnava, 2000; 2002). *Checkpoints* (Varnava, 2000; 2002) is a series of publications aimed at facilitating institutional self-audit regarding a school's non-violence promotion using checklists and web diagrams. The findings suggested that certain cultural, organizational and managerial factors could either enhance or reduce a school's ability to engage with changes that promote self-audit. Indeed, some schools were more ready to embrace organizational change than were others, and thus more ready to implement a self-evaluation. The findings suggested that the process of conducting a needs analysis could be understood in terms of three levels of *readiness* (see Figure 4.2).

Models   Key Characteristics

Circular Model
The school clearly articulates its educational vision
The school ethos is explicit through all areas of school life
Emphasis is placed on children's participation and empowerment
Emphasis on the wider curriculum and emotional literacy
Places value in children's social time outside the classroom to enhance learning across the school day
A responsive and reflexive leadership and management style
The school displays good knowledge of its strengths and weaknesses and can prioritise targets
Strives for consistency between behaviour policy and practice
An emphasis on communication and dynamic relationships with children, staff, parents,
    governors and the wider community
Training and development is linked to the school review process
The school rationalises and selects from initiatives at both national and local level

Corkscrew Model
The school shares its educational vision
The school ethos not always made explicit
Emphasis is placed on children's participation
Emphasis on the wider curriculum and emotional literacy
An absence of supportive strategies that value children's time outside the classroom
A pragmatic 'Quick fix' style of management
The behaviour policy facilitates the review of practice
An emphasis on communication with some evidence of parental support and community links
Training as a mechanism for change and self-reflection
The school selects from initiatives at both national and local level

String Model
The school has difficulty in articulating its educational vision
The school ethos is not explicit
Emphasis is placed on academic achievement and the formal curriculum
Little emphasis is placed on the supportive strategies that value children's time outside the
    classroom
A strategic or autocratic style of management
Inconsistencies between behaviour policy and practice
Limited evidence of systems and policies for the management of pupils and staff in effective
    communication between staff and professional isolation
Limited evidence of home/school/community links
The school has difficulty selecting from initiatives at national and local level and tends to
    become overloaded

Figure 4.2 Levels of readiness.
Source: Jennifer and Shaughnessy, 2005

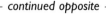
continued opposite

Case Study 4.1 continued

The *Circular level* reflects an organization that is self-aware and responsive, operating from a clearly focused rationale. The school is able to prioritize its course of action and is aware of the need for constant review and evaluation of practice. The school culture could be characterized as democratic, with a focus on children's participation in decision-making. The school recognizes the negative consequences of not addressing the issues of bullying and violence and is committed to the process of change. A school operating from this level of readiness is likely to implement a thorough needs analysis as an integral part of the School Development Plan. A school conducting a needs analysis from this level of readiness is likely to put a great deal of effort into actively involving the whole-school community (staff, pupils, parents, governors and the wider community) resulting in a sense of ownership of the process of carrying out a needs analysis.

The *Corkscrew level* reflects an organizational culture that fluctuates. The school is sometimes able to identify action through self-reflection but the action is not always clearly focused. The school culture could be characterized as pragmatic, with some emphasis on children's participation. While the school acknowledges the existence of bullying and violence, takes ownership of the problem and identifies some of the negative aspects of its presence, it is ambivalent about committing to the process of change. A school operating from this level of readiness is likely either to feel complacent about the issue of bullying and violence or to feel ambivalent about conducting a needs analysis.

The *String level* reflects a fragile organizational culture. A school operating from this perspective has limited self-evaluation skills and experiences difficulty in articulating a clear course of action. The school culture could be characterized as strategic and autocratic with little emphasis placed on children and young people's participation. The school is not yet sensitive to the bullying and violence experienced by their children and young people; however, others may be aware of a problem, for example, parents or the wider community. A school operating from this level of readiness is unlikely to have much success with conducting a needs analysis. Potential difficulties with conducting a needs analysis at this level include lack of explicit support for the exercise by the senior management team and even sabotage.

Establishing a Working Group

Prior to carrying out a needs analysis it is necessary to establish a working group to share the planning, advise and manage the process, and measure the outcomes of the ongoing intervention. A working group should include young people (for example, School Council representatives), staff (for example, head teacher, Personal, Social and Health Education (PSHE) coordinator, head of year), non-teaching staff (for example, school nurse, school caretaker, lunchtime supervisors), parents, school governors, and representatives from the wider community (for example, the police, health visitor). Once you have read this chapter, please start thinking about forming a working group in your school and complete the working group form (see Activity Handout 4.1, p. 48). Once you've formed a working group you are ready to develop a working group contract (see Chapter 5, Activity 5.1) and start collecting information on the setting and the people (see Needs Analysis Step 1, p. 35).

Activities for the Training Event

Activity 4.1 What Do We Mean by a Needs Analysis? (90 minutes)

Purpose
• To promote a clear understanding of what a needs analysis is.

Materials
  Flip chart paper and pens
  Activity Handout 4.2 What do we mean by a needs analysis? See p. 49.

Procedure
Divide the group into subgroups of four, ensuring that each group comprises a mix of participants, that is, pupils, teachers and parents. Ask each member of the group to think of one main issue regarding bullying and violence that they consider important to change and address in their school and ask a representative from each subgroup to write these down on a piece of flip chart paper. In subgroups, participants should discuss the issues written down by the representative. During the discussion, the participants should identify which issues are common and which are different for members of their subgroup and make a summary of their findings (note that at this stage participants should not be seeking/offering solutions to the issues raised). Allow 20–30 minutes for this. Prompt questions could include:

• *What is the nature of the bullying and violence problems experienced by young people in your school?*
• *How do you know that these are problems faced by young people in your school?*
• *What positive anti-bullying and behaviour management policies and practices are currently in place in your school?*
• *Where do you need to take further action?*

Ask representatives from each subgroup, in turn, to report their ideas to the main group. On a flip chart, the facilitator should summarize the range of issues identified. The main point to raise at this stage is that while subgroups will have identified common issues, individual members of each subgroup may well perceive them through a slightly different lens.

Ask the subgroups to consider how they would manage a whole-school community needs analysis, that is, what does each subgroup care about and what do they want to change? Allow 20–30 minutes for this. Prompt questions could include:

- *Who will be involved in the needs analysis?*
- *What will be the focus of the needs analysis, that is, what issues identified in the first part of this activity do you intend to address?*
- *Why have you selected these specific issues to address?*
- *What information will be collected?*
- *What methods will be used to collect such information? (For example, school statistics, such as, bullying and violent incident records, absence figures; written documents, such as anti-bullying and behaviour policies; observations in a variety of areas such as classrooms, playgrounds, corridors; questionnaires, focus groups and interviews)*
- *Who/where will this information be collected from?*

Discussion

Discussion with the whole group is essential if all participants are to reach an understanding of what a needs analysis entails. Ask representatives from each group, in turn, to report their ideas to the main group. The facilitator should list the main ideas on a flip chart under each of the prompt questions outlined above. One of the main points to raise is that each of the subgroups (and individuals within subgroups!) will have a different understanding of what the focus of the needs analysis should be which, in turn, will impact on the goals, the potential difficulties, the methods for data collection and, ultimately, if differences cannot be resolved, the efficacy of the intervention. It is also important that participants are aware that while subgroups (and individuals within subgroups) might identify different areas on which to focus, they are all equally valid.

Activity 4.2 Saboteur (15 minutes) *(adapted from Pretty et al., 1995)*

Purpose
- To show how communication and group work can be easily disrupted.
- To create a group strategy for recognizing and dealing with sabotage.

Materials
   Groups of three chairs.
   Flip chart and pens.
   Post-it notes.

Procedure
Divide participants into groups of three. Within each subgroup, they have to fill three roles – the speaker, the listener and the saboteur. The speaker

and listener face each other to talk, while the saboteur can move and talk. The speaker is asked to describe some aspect of their work or life to the listener. The saboteur is asked to try to sabotage (that is, disrupt) this discussion in any non-violent manner. Roaming saboteurs can move between groups. These may be the facilitator, plus any other participants who did not join groups when the full group was divided. After two minutes, ask participants to change roles. Then, again, after two more minutes, as it is essential for all participants to have the opportunity to play all three roles. Everybody should know what it feels like to be a saboteur and to be sabotaged.

Discussion

Discussion after this activity is essential. To establish a group strategy, it is necessary to get participants to reflect on how they felt:

- *What was it like to be a saboteur and to be sabotaged?*
- *Did you find it easy or difficult to disrupt the conversation?*

Then ask everyone to write out the different types of saboteur they experienced or have experienced in the past on a Post-it note, and stick them on a flip chart. Examples include dominance, rigidity, interruptions (answers/ questions), joking and not being serious, rudeness, silence, taking over with enthusiasm and physical distraction by fidgeting.

Then ask participants to reflect upon ways to deal with such sabotage, that is, sabotaging saboteurs:

- *How have you or could you deal with saboteurs?*
- *What are the ways groups can deal with saboteur individuals?*

Write these strategies on another sheet. Examples include: ignore politely, polite/clear interruption, stop the discussion, talk it out (publicly or personally), acknowledge and postpone, divert attention – form subgroups or set a task, use the saboteur for debate, ask others for help, allow it, walk away. These can be stuck on the wall for all to see and can be referred to during the rest of the session.

This activity and discussion may be especially useful if there are particularly disruptive members of the group. Such an activity may be an opportunity for them to reflect on their behaviour and for the group to develop ways of dealing with the disruption. It can also prepare participants for potentially difficult situations during the needs analysis. More importantly, however, it introduces the idea of sabotage to the whole group, as well as focusing on strategies to deal with it. During the rest of the session, it is likely that participants will self-regulate without any facilitator input needed. Any group interruption will be greeted by calls of 'sabotage'.

Activity 4.3 Problems and Solutions (45 minutes) *(adapted from Pretty et al., 1995)*

Purpose
- To give participants the opportunity to discuss real problems they face or will face in conducting a needs analysis and to generate potential solutions.
- To emphasize equality in power and authority within the group.
- To encourage participants to share problems and actively seek experiences and suggestions from each other.
- To highlight that participants all have relevant and valuable experience.

Materials
Two sets of five or six chairs arranged in two concentric circles, the inside ones facing the outside.
A watch or electronic timer to time each round.
Object to make a noise, for example, bell, cup and spoon.

Procedure
Ask participants to reflect on particular problems they will face or have faced. This could include:

- *problems in carrying out a needs analysis;*
- *problems/difficulties likely to be faced when returning to their own departments.*

Then ask participants to sit in any seat. Instruct them that those sitting in the inside circle will be the consultants or solution-suggesters. Those sitting on the outside facing in will be the clients or the problem-presenters. Explain that each pair has three minutes to discuss problems and potential solutions. After three minutes, the outside circle rotates by one chair, bringing a new client to face each consultant. Give another three minutes for discussion of problems and solutions. This continues for all five or six people in the circles. Then give two minutes for all clients and consultants to write down a summary of problems and solutions. After this is completed, the clients and consultants change circles and reverse roles. The activity is repeated.

Discussion
Inform participants that they may discuss private as well as public problems. You could give an example from your own experience to demonstrate this. No one but the consultant will get to hear of them, as there is no presentation to the whole group after the activity. This activity usually generates highly animated discussion. It is important that individuals do write down a summary of the problems and potential solutions. These can then be used in

a follow-up discussion, such as in the elaboration of detailed implementation or action plans. An extra learning point can be made if participants are asked to choose one problem to present to each consultant. During the discussion, the facilitator can discuss how the problem presented initially changed as the client became more aware of the real issues after each consultation. This activity also highlights how a group approach to problems and solutions can generate more ideas than one individual can alone.

Further Reading

Ainscow, M., Hopkins, D., Southworth, G. and West, M. (1994) *Creating the Conditions for School Improvement*. London: Fulton.

Cowie, H., Boardman, C., Dawkins, J. and Jennifer, D. (2004) *Emotional Health and Well-Being: A Practical Guide for Schools*. London: Sage Publications.

Davis, R. (1995) 'From data to action', in M. Lloyd-Smith and J. Dwyfor-Davies (eds), *On the Margins*. Stoke-on-Trent: Trentham Books. pp. 167–79.

Dusenbury, L., Falco, M., Lake, A., Brannigan, R. and Bosworth, K. (1997) 'Nine critical elements of promising violence prevention programs', *Journal of School Health*, 67(10): 409–14.

Gray, J., Reynolds, D., Wilcox, B., Farrell, S. and Jesson, D. (1999) *Improving Schools: Performance and Potential*. Buckingham: Open University Press.

Harris, A. (2002) 'Effective leadership in schools facing challenging contexts', *School Leadership and Management*, 22(1): 15–26.

Hopkins, D., Harris, A. and Jackson, D. (1997) 'Understanding the school's capacity for development: Growth stages and strategies', *School Leadership and Management*, 17(3): 401–11.

Jennifer, D. and Shaughnessy, J. (2005) 'Promoting non-violence in schools: the role of cultural, organisational and managerial factors', *Educational and Child Psychology*, 22(3): 58–66.

Muijs, D., Harris, A., Chapman, C., Stoll, L. and Russ, J. (2004) 'Improving schools in socioeconomically disadvantaged areas – a review of the research evidence', *School Effectiveness and School Improvement*, 15(2): 149–75.

Potter, D., Reynolds, D. and Chapman, C. (2002) 'School improvement for schools facing challenging circumstances: A review of research and practice', *School Leadership and Management*, 22(3): 243–56.

Stoll, L. and Myers, K. (1998) *No Quick Fixes*. London: Falmer Press.

Websites

Cowie, H. and Jennifer, D., et al. (2007) *School Bullying and Violence: Taking Action*, www.vista-europe.org

National College for School Leadership, www.ncsl.org.uk

UK Observatory for the Promotion of Non-Violence, www.ukobservatory.com

Evaluation Tools

The Hertfordshire Framework for School Self-Evaluation, www.thegrid.org.uk/leadership/sse/

Confronting Conflict in Schools Audit. Leap Confronting Conflict, 8 Lennox Road, London, N4 3NW. +44 (0) 20 7272 5630, www.leaplinx.com/youth/schools.htm

Her Majesty's Inspectorate of Education (HMIE) (2002) *How Good is Our School?* www.hmie.gov.uk/publication.asp

National Healthy School Standard (NHSS), www.wiredforhealth.gov.uk/cat.php?catid=966&docid=7479

School Self-Evaluation, www.sheu.org.uk/survey/sse.htm

Scottish Office Education Department/Her Majesty's Inspectorate of Education (SOEID/HMIE). (1992) *Using Ethos Indicators in Primary School Self-Evaluation: Taking Account of the Views of Pupils, Parents and Teachers*, www.ethosnet.co.uk

Scottish Office Education Department/Her Majesty's Inspectorate of Education (1992) (SOEID/HMIE) *Using Ethos Indicators in Secondary School Self-Evaluation: Taking Account of the Views of Pupils, Parents and Teachers*, www.ethosnet.co.uk

Varnava, G. (2005) *Checkpoints for Schools: Towards a Non-violent Society.* London: NSPCC. A copy of the document can be downloaded from www.nspcc.org.uk/Inform/TrainingAndConsultancy/Consultancy/SupportingProductsAndResources/CheckpointsForSchools_asp_ifega234 28.html

Wirral Health Promoting Schools Scheme. Health Links, 49 Hamilton Square, Birkenhead, CH41 5AR. Tel: +44 (0) 151 647 0211, www.wirralhealth.org.uk/healthlinks/youth.asp

Activity Handout 4.1

Needs Analysis Working Group			
Name	Role	Signature	Date

Date of first meeting ....

Activity Handout 4.2 What Do We Mean By a Needs Analysis?

Part 1

- What is the nature of the bullying and violence problems experienced by young people in your school?
- How do you know that these are problems faced by young people in your school?
- What positive anti-bullying and behaviour management policies and practices are currently in place in your school?
- Where do you need to take further action?

Part 2

- Who will be involved in the needs analysis?
- What will be the focus of the needs analysis, that is, what issues identified in the first part of this activity do you intend to address?
- Why have you selected these specific issues to address?
- What information will be collected?
- What methods will be used to collect such information? (For example, school statistics, such as bullying and violent incident records, absence figures; written documents, such as anti-bullying and behaviour policies; observations in a variety of areas such as classrooms, playgrounds, corridors; questionnaires, focus groups and interviews)
- Who/where will this information be collected from?

5 | Conducting a needs analysis

Objectives

- To provide readers with a selection of ideas, tools and resources with which to carry out an effective needs analysis.
- To enable readers to develop a working group contract.

What Information Will You Require for Your Needs Analysis?

The aim of this chapter is to provide readers with some practical ideas and tools for carrying out a needs analysis in order to gain a full understanding of the issue of bullying and violence in your school prior to implementing an intervention.

The information that you collect during your needs analysis can be drawn from four main sources:

- documentary evidence relevant to the prevention and reduction of school bullying and violence, such as copies of the School Development Plan, copies of school policies (such as behaviour management, anti-bullying, communication, equal opportunities, child protection, PSHE and Citizenship) and the curriculum;
- school-based data, such as bullying and violent incident records, annual absence records, annual exclusion records and the percentage of pupils on the special educational needs register;
- questionnaires, interviews and focus groups with representatives from all sections of the school community, that is, pupils, teaching and non-teaching staff, parents/carers and governors;
- observations in a variety of settings, including classrooms, entrance hall and corridors, outside spaces at break and lunchtime, inside spaces at break and lunchtime, dining hall, toilets and assembly (Galvin, 2006).

What Methods are Available for Carrying Out a Needs Analysis?

There is a wide range of methods available to measure bullying and violence in your school, including questionnaire surveys, interviews, focus group discussions, observations and structured research activities.

Questionnaire surveys are a useful way of providing a broad picture of the nature and scale of the problem of bullying and violence in your school. For example, they can be used to find out about the general quality of the school climate (see Chapter 10) or about the frequency and nature of bullying and violent incidents in particular (see below). If the questionnaires are essentially the same for all representatives of the school community (that is, pupils, teachers and non-teaching staff, parents/carers and governors) comparisons of the results from each group can be meaningfully made and the variations in responses examined.

Either, schools can choose to use previously published questionnaires or, they can decide to design their own (see Box 5.1). The advantage of designing your own questionnaire is that pupils can be involved at an early stage of the needs analysis. Not only will this help to raise awareness about bullying and violence, it enables young people to appreciate the effects of the survey and to take it more seriously (Sharp et al., 1994). A second advantage is that the questionnaire can be tailor-made to meet the specific needs of your school. However, the main disadvantage of designing your own measure is the need to pilot it and test it out, which can be very time-consuming. On the other hand, there are several tried and tested questionnaires available, the use of which will enable you to compare the results easily with those of other schools.

Box 5.1 Considerations for questionnaire design

1 When to use a questionnaire
   You should use a questionnaire when you have a relatively large number of participants and when you want to measure, for example, facts (age, year group), behaviour (types of bullying), coping strategies and attitudes.

2 Advantages
   Questionnaires are relatively quick and inexpensive to administer, and can be kept anonymous and confidential.

3 Disadvantages
   With questionnaires, responses are fixed, rendering responsiveness to each individual's experience impossible.

4 Asking the 'wrong' questions
   Avoid double-barrelled questions, for example, 'Are records of complaints kept and is a regular survey carried out to inform policy?' Double-barrelled questions ask two questions at once and can be confusing, therefore, split into separate questions. Avoid ambiguous questions, for example, 'How do

continued opposite

Box 5.1 continued

you teach about violence through the curriculum?' by taking care with sentence structure. Avoid leading questions, for example, 'Do you agree that bullying and violence are a big problem in your school?' Be aware that leading questions encourage a particular answer, that is, 'yes' or 'no'. Avoid negatively framed questions as they are often difficult to understand, for example, 'Violent language and name-calling are not encouraged. Agree/disagree?' 'Violent language and name-calling are discouraged. Agree/disagree?' avoids the problem. In addition, questions should be kept as short as possible as they are easier to understand and the language should be kept simple with jargon avoided.

5   Asking the right questions
    When designing your questionnaire you will need to keep a clear focus on the aims of your needs analysis.

6   Choosing a question format
    While there is no absolutely correct or incorrect way to word a question, leading questions lead the respondent to answer 'yes' or 'no', whereas an open-ended question that uses what? when? where? who? why? or how? opens up the response. Your choice of question format will depend on the stage of the needs analysis, the specific topic under investigation and the context. On the one hand, open-ended questions allow rich detail, although they are difficult to code and analyse. On the other, closed questions are simple and quick, and easier to code, analyse and report.

7   Choosing a response format
    Your chosen response scale must be balanced, exhaustive and able to facilitate 'don't know' and 'other'. There are a number of response formats to choose from, including:

(a) Simple response
    What is your gender?   Male   Female

(b) Checklist
    Which of the following policy documents do you have in place?

Behaviour Management Policy	[ ]	Anti-Bullying Policy	[ ]
Communication Policy	[ ]	Equal Opportunities Policy	[ ]
Child Protection Policy	[ ]	PSHE Policy	[ ]
Citizenship Policy	[ ]		

(c) Ranking scale
    Please rank these school locations in order of where you feel most safe in school (1 would be most safe, 10 would be least)

Playground/school field	[ ]	Hallways/stairwells	[ ]
In class with the teacher present	[ ]	Classroom (no teacher)	[ ]
In a PE class/changing rooms	[ ]	In the toilets	[ ]
In the dining room	[ ]	To and from school	[ ]
At the bus stop	[ ]	On the school bus	[ ]

continued overleaf

Box 5.1 continued

(d) Rating scale
   How important to you is the presence of a peer support system in your school?
   (please circle)
   1   2   3   4   5   6   7
   Not at all important   Very important

(e) Likert Scale
   Children who bully should be expelled
   Strongly agree Agree Neither agree or disagree Disagree Strongly disagree

8 Finally, you will need to consider the length of your questionnaire and the
   time it will take to complete. You will also need to include clear and polite
   instructions on how to complete the questionnaire, together with
   assurances of anonymity and confidentiality.

The most commonly used measures for studying the incidence and prevalence of school bullying include self-report, peer nomination and teacher nomination questionnaires. For example, the 'Life in School checklist' (Arora and Thompson, 1999) can be used to gauge the extent of bullying behaviours, other aggressive behaviours and friendly behaviours in a school during the preceding week. The *Revised Olweus Bully/Victim Questionnaire* (Olweus, 1996) provides a measure of the incidence of bullying, and others' reactions to bullying, with children of 8 years old and above, over the past two or three months. For younger participants, Smith and Levan (1995) have devised a pictorial questionnaire for use with children aged 6 to 7, to explore their perceptions and experiences of bullying. Peer nomination scales have also been developed to capture information about the group context within which bullying takes place. For example, the *Participant Role Scale* has been designed for use with 12- and 13-year-olds to investigate participant roles (victims, bullies, assistants, reinforcers, outsiders, defenders) in the bullying process (Salmivalli et al., 1996). Not only do questionnaires highlight specific issues at this stage of the needs analysis, they can also be used as tools for review and evaluation at a later stage of the process.

On the other hand, semi-structured interviews will allow you to obtain more detailed and richer information about certain aspects of school life than may be possible with a questionnaire survey. A second advantage is that interviews enable all participants, irrespective of age, ethnic minority, literacy or disability level, to be involved meaningfully in the consultation process. Third, interviews offer both the opportunity to access sensitive material, and the opportunity to be responsive to each individual participant's experience. Box 5.2 offers some considerations for designing a semi-structured interview.

Group interviews, or focus groups, are also advantageous as they offer participants the opportunity to develop their ideas through collaborative discussion. Indeed, focus groups have a number of distinct advantages over interviews for gathering certain types of qualitative data. First, they offer support to individuals, enabling participants the opportunity for greater openness. Second, a focus group does not have to be terminated when a participant does not respond. Third, there is reduced pressure on individual participants to respond to every question. Fourth, they are flexible in that they can be used alone or in combination with other research methods (see Box 5.4). Finally, the cost of conducting a focus group is less than conducting an interview with the same number of participants. Furthermore, focus groups are particularly appropriate for use with children and young people. For example, they offer an effective and versatile means of exploring experiences and perceptions on a wide range of issues with children as young as 8 years old and replicate group work typical of the school experience (Mauthner, 1997). In addition, focus groups encourage open discussion of sensitive issues (for example, bullying and violence in school) and allow for the exploration of unanticipated issues as they arise in the discussion in a safe environment. Furthermore, the support provided by the small group setting may help to reduce the power differential between adult researcher and young participant, and the presence and contribution of other children may encourage participants to express their own opinions (Hill et al., 1996).

Box 5.2 Considerations for semi-structured interview design

1 When to use a semi-structured interview
   You should use a semi-structured interview when you want to find out detailed information about bullying and violence in your school, such as, the processes and dynamics of bullying situations and the group context within which it takes place.

2 Advantages
   Semi-structured interviews offer a flexible and adaptable means of finding things out since questions can clarify and probe participants' responses. Lines of enquiry can be modified according to each individual interview and non-verbal cues, such as body language, may help to deepen your understanding of verbal responses.

3 Disadvantages
   One-to-one interviewing is heavy on resources, including human, financial and time resources.

4 Asking the 'wrong' questions
   The same considerations apply as for questionnaire design (see Box 5.1).

5 Asking the right questions
   Open-ended questions are probably most commonly used in interviews as

continued overleaf

Box 5.2 continued

they allow for greater flexibility, for example, they allow for exploration of issues in more depth, allow for clarification of issues raised, encourage cooperation and rapport, and may produce unexpected or challenging answers.

6 Sequence of questions
An interview schedule for a semi-structured interview is likely to include:
(a) introductory comments (usually scripted), including introductions, explanation of the nature and purpose of the interview, assurances of confidentiality, permission to audio tape record the interview and/or make notes;
(b) a list of topic headings with key questions under each heading;
(c) a set of related prompt questions;
(d) closing comments, including thank you and goodbye.

The actions and behaviour of pupils and adults in your school are central to gaining an understanding about the issue of bullying and violence. Naturalistic observations, therefore, provide a useful opportunity to identify what is happening. A major advantage of observation is its directness and the opportunity it offers to observe real-life phenomena, such as bullying and violence in school, as they occur in their natural social contexts (Cowie et al., 2002). Indeed, observational studies provide the means for gathering naturalistic information regarding children and young people's involvement in aggressive and violent behaviour that can extend knowledge about bullying and violence in school beyond that gained from other methods (Boulton, 1995). For example, observational data gathered on the playground or in the classroom regarding how pupils respond to bullying situations highlight the discrepancy between what individuals claim they would do in questionnaires and interviews if they were involved in a bullying situation, with what they actually do in a real-life bullying situation (Ólafsson and Jóhannsdóttir, 2004).

Nevertheless, observational methods are also very resource-consuming, requiring commitment in terms of financial, human and time resources. Furthermore, by their very design, observational studies can only capture a fraction of what goes on, to the exclusion of other activities that occur either before or after the episode under observation (Cowie et al., 2002). Moreover, when observing bullying behaviours, direct physical aggression (for example, pushing, hitting, punching, kicking) and direct verbal aggression (for example, yelling abuse at another, name-calling, using insulting expressions, making verbal threats) are more easily observed than indirect aggression (for example, spreading malicious rumours about another, excluding a person from the group, disclosing another's secrets to a third person). Box 5.3 presents considerations for carrying out observations.

Box 5.3 Considerations for carrying out observations

1 First of all, you will need to decide how you define bullying, that is, you will need to think about what types of behaviours you are going to observe.
2 Decide on your sample, that is, think about who you are going to observe. For example, are you going to observe bullies and victims, or do you consider that bullying extends beyond individual children to include the wider peer group?
3 Decide when and where you are going to make your observations.
4 Decide upon how you are going to record and code your observations.

In the spirit of the Children's Act (2004) and the UN *Convention on the Rights of the Child* (1989), we recommend that opportunities should be given to young people to express their views and opinions in a variety of ways including interviews, focus groups and class discussions to provide a more in-depth perspective. For example, an effective method of carrying out research with children is to combine interviews and focus group discussions with structured research activities to stimulate discussion (see Box 5.4 for examples). The use of structured activities is particularly appropriate for gathering information from children and young people. Such activities capitalize upon children's strengths rather than their weaknesses, thereby allowing children with different competencies and preferences to take part (Clark, 2004). They can be used with children of different ages and abilities, and can be adapted to suit different languages and cultures. They provide children with space and time to think about what they want to express, and talk freely about issues that concern them, without creating pressure for them to respond quickly with the 'correct' answer (Punch 2002). Further, the use of structured activities helps create a relaxed atmosphere, and rapport, which is therefore likely to increase participants' confidence and encourage children to talk more freely and honestly.

Box 5.4 Examples of structured research activities

• Cartoons and drawings of bullying scenarios can be used to elicit children's and young people's views on a range of issues regarding bullying and violence in school including definitions, types of behaviour, moral reasoning, and coping strategies.
• Children's drawings accompanied by storytelling prompted by open-ended questions can be used to find out about their knowledge and experience of bullying and violence at school.
• The 'draw and write' technique can be productively used with children as young as 6 years old to help them focus on a particular issue.
• Letter-writing can be used to find out about whether pupils have ever had any problems with their friends at school or know of someone who has.

continued overleaf

Box 5.4 continued

Participants are asked to write about a bullying problem as if writing to their best friend, to include details about what happened, why they believe it happened, how they felt, what they did about it, and how it was resolved (or not as the case may be).

• Through drawing mental maps of the school and identifying areas where bullying and violence occurs, in subsequent discussion, children and young people can provide a perspective of the phenomenon that adult observations might otherwise miss.

• Photo diaries of school life and the school environment also provide children with the opportunity to represent aspects of bullying and violence in school without the effect of adult influence.

• The quality circle method described by Cowie and Sharp (1994) offers a curriculum-based, participative problem-solving approach, which provides pupils with the opportunity to explore the issues of bullying and violence in their school, together with a clear structure to formulate and implement their own solutions.

Alternatively, children and young people can be actively involved in the needs analysis process as peer researchers. There are a number of ways in which children and young people can be involved, ranging from decision-makers/consultants to active researchers carrying out the research tasks. Box 5.5 presents some ideas for how children and young people can be involved.

Box 5.5 Involving children and young people as peer researchers

• Recruit a group of children and young people as pupil representatives to form part of the working group responsible for overseeing the needs analysis.

• Give children and young people the opportunity to be involved in identifying the issues to be explored in the needs analysis and designing a set of shared goals.

• Take account of children's and young people's views in designing appropriate research tools and methods, for example, questionnaires and interviews.

• Train a group of children and young people in data-collection methods, for example, in conducting questionnaire surveys, group discussions and interviews

• Give children and young people the opportunity to be involved in analysing data and interpreting findings.

• Give children and young people the opportunity to be involved in disseminating the findings, for example, in writing up the report, producing a poster of the findings, distributing reports, making presentations and speaking to the media.

Consulting with children and young people in the needs analysis process, and indeed involving them as peer researchers, requires considera-tion of a number of ethical issues in respect of their rights such as privacy and confidentiality. Using a child's rights-based approach to show how the ethics of justice and respect relate to projects with children of all ages, Alderson and Morrow (2004) offer a practical book on the ethics of consulting with children and young people.

Why Are Review and Evaluation Important?

The major purpose of review and evaluation processes is to determine whether the intervention has made a difference. Prior to asking 'Does it work?' it is important to establish what 'it' is and that 'it' has actually been implemented. Therefore, before evaluating the effectiveness of your chosen intervention, it is important to review its implementation. The aim of the review is to determine the extent to which the intervention has been put into practice, including those aspects of the intervention that are working well and those aspects of the intervention that need attention. The results of the review process will provide information that will enable you to make amendments to the intervention, prior to its being evaluated for effectiveness. In addition to providing information about implementation and effectiveness, review and evaluation also provide the opportunity for supplying information to potential funders, and for sharing and disseminating good practice.

Evaluation should therefore have three major purposes:

- to review the implementation of the intervention;
- to evaluate the effectiveness of the intervention;
- to evaluate key characteristics of the intervention (Riley and Segal, 2002).

Activities for the Training Event

Activity 5.1 Working Group Contract (60 minutes) (adapted from Pretty et al., 1995)

Purpose
- To develop a working group contract.
- To develop norms for group behaviour.

Materials
   Activity Handout 5.1 What Would You Do If? See p. 65.
   Notebooks and pens.
   Flip chart and pens.

Procedure
Divide the group into small groups of up to five people. Hand out Activity Handout 5.1. If you have more than one group, allocate specific questions to each group (see Activity Handout 5.1, p. 65). Ask groups to consider what they would do if they encountered these problems in their needs analysis.

After about 45 minutes, when each group has considered their strategy for dealing with each problem, ask them to report back to the large group. To help the facilitator guide the group into developing a working group contract, the facilitator lists on a flip chart the main ideas and strategies for addressing each problem. When all the problems have been discussed, including comments from other subgroups, ask each subgroup to agree a team contract among themselves. This working group contract is based on the activity and discussions, and will serve as a code of conduct for participants' working group in their school. After the team contracts have been made, encourage everyone to make a record for future reference.

Discussion
The questions should contain a mix of problems relating to both group dynamics and difficulties related to carrying out a needs analysis. The success of this exercise lies in anticipating problems related to carrying out a needs analysis before they occur. Discussion is usually most animated among participants who have previous experience as they will be able to illustrate problems and strategies with stories from their past. Having the contract in their notebooks means that problematic working group members can be encouraged simply to look at and stick to their contract, rather than other members finding it necessary to confront them directly with their behaviour. These 'rules' help to guide the working groups through small crises as members ask each other to 'remember rule 8!' or to simply say 'group contract'.

Activity 5.2 Brainstorming and Setting Priorities (30 minutes)
(adapted from Pretty et al., 1995)

Purpose
• To generate issues, topics and questions in preparation for a needs analysis.
• To group, sort, rank ideas in order to set priorities for the initial consultation.
• To demonstrate a method of reaching consensus.
• To help with team-building.

Materials
　Flip charts, flip chart pens.

Procedure
In small groups of three to four participants, use brainstorming to generate issues, topics and questions that they want to address in their needs analysis. Encourage the groups to think adventurously. Everything must be included, even the most outlandish and wild ideas! Encourage quantity rather than quality: the more ideas the better. Each member of the group writes down a series of ideas, issues and questions on Post-it notes and places on the flip chart. The Post-it notes are clustered either by one or by

a number of volunteers or by all of the participants in each group. Exact duplicates may be removed but all other Post-its must remain, even the most outrageous. Each group must agree on how the Post-its are to be clustered; this can form the basis for the subdivision of a needs analysis into theme areas. The group writes the themes on the flip chart.

Discussion
Participants find it very difficult not to comment on or evaluate ideas generated in a brainstorming exercise. Emphasize that all judgements must be ruled out until after all ideas have been generated. This method is quite flexible and can be used for a variety of purposes, including developing and revising an interview checklist or a focus group schedule, comparing the strengths and weaknesses of various interventions, preparing a working group contract, and so on.

Activity 5.3 Matching Issue and Method (60 minutes) (*adapted from Pretty et al., 1995*)

Purpose
- To encourage participants to think critically about the possible application of different methods for data collection in their needs analysis.
- To help participants plan their needs analysis.
- To enhance group dynamics.

Materials
  Checklist of questions/issues generated in Activity 5.2.

Procedure
Before conducting a needs analysis, each working group must discuss how it plans to explore the issues highlighted in the checklist generated in the Setting Priorities exercise. This will happen at every stage of the needs analysis when new questions and issues arise. To encourage a diverse use of a range of methods, a matching issue and method session is very useful. Divide the group into small groups. Take the checklist developed in the brainstorming and Setting Priorities activity and divide the issues among the small groups. Ask each group to identify, and make a note of, what kind of information they would need to collect that would be effective for exploring each issue/topic/question on the checklist, who or where they would need to collect the information from, and which method, or variation of it, would be the most appropriate/effective. Ask each small group to present their findings, inviting other small groups to add their ideas and inspire each other.

Discussion
The exercise on linking issues to methods can be a very important turning point in the training as it compels participants to start making links

between what they have learnt and putting it into practice. After exposing participants to a wide range of methods in this chapter, they can then explore how to use them to address real-world issues. It is a good time to get participants to reflect upon the rich variety of methods available and to realize that a variety of methods (triangulation) can be used to address each issue, topic and question. Conversely, particular issues or questions demand specific methods.

Further Reading

Cowie, H., Boardman, C., Dawkins, J. and Jennifer, D. (2004) *Emotional Health and Well-Being: A Practical Guide for Schools*. London: Sage Publications.

France, A. (2000) *Involving Young People in Research Projects*. York: Joseph Rowntree Foundation.

Kirby, P. (1999) *Involving Young People in Research*. York: Joseph Rowntree Foundation.

Robson, C. (2002) *Real World Research*. Oxford: Blackwell.

Sharp, S., and Smith, P.K. (eds) (1994) *Tackling Bullying in Your School: A Practical Handbook for Teachers*. London: Routledge.

Warrall, S. (2000) *Young People as Researchers: A Learning Resource Pack*. London: Save the Children.

Websites

Cowie, H. and Jennifer, D. et al. (2007) *School Bullying and Violence: Taking Action*, www.vista-europe.org

Department for Education and Skills, www.dfes.gov.uk/bullying

European Year of Citizenship through Education 2005, www.citizenship-bg.org/en/programme.html

National College for School Leadership, www.ncsl.org.uk

State Agency for Child Protection and Child Protection Policy, www.sacp.government.bg/index_en.htm

Teachernet, www.teachernet.gov.uk

UK Observatory for the Promotion of Non-Violence, www.ukobservatory.com

Evaluation Studies

Cartwright, N. (2005) 'Setting up and sustaining peer support systems in a range of schools over 20 years', *Pastoral Care in Education*, 23(2): 45–50.

Jennifer, D. and Shaughnessy, J. (2004) 'Is your school ready to tackle the emotional issues around change?', *Emotional Literacy Update*, 7: 8–9.

Naylor, P. (2000) 'Elliott Durham School's anti-bullying peer support system: A case study of good practice in a secondary school', in H. Cowie and P. Wallace (eds), *Peer Support in Action*. London: Sage Publications. pp. 36–48.

Naylor, P., and Cowie, H. (1999) 'The effectiveness of peer support systems in challenging school bullying: the perspectives and experiences of teachers and pupils', *Journal of Adolescence*, 22(4): 1–13.

Smith, P.K. (2003). *Evaluation of the DfES Anti-Bullying Pack. Research Brief No: RBX06–03*, www.dfes.gov.uk/bullying/

Smith, P.K., Ananiadou, K. and Cowie, H. (2003) 'Interventions to reduce school bullying', *Canadian Journal of Psychiatry*, 48(9): 591–9.

Stevens, V., de Bourdeaudhuij, I. and van Oost, P. (2000) 'Bullying in Flemish schools: an evaluation of anti-bullying intervention in primary and secondary schools', *British Journal of Educational Psychology*, 70: 195–210.

Watt, S. and Higgins, C. (1999) 'Using behaviour management packages as a stepping stone from school to society: a Scottish evaluation of Turn Your School Round', *Children & Society*, 1: 346–64.

Resources: **Questionnaires**

Dahlberg, L.L., Toal, S.B., Swahn, M. and Behrens, C.B. (2005) *Measuring Violence-Related Attitudes, Behaviors, and Influences Among Youths: A Compendium of Assessment Tools*. Atlanta, GA: Centers for Disease Control and Prevention.

Frederickson, N. and Cameron, R.J. (series eds) and S. Sharp (vol. ed.) (1999) *Bullying Behaviour in Schools: Psychology in Education Portfolio*. Windsor: NFER NELSON. (This volume provides a selection of questionnaires.)

Resources: **Evaluation Tools**

ABA Bullying Audit Toolkit http://www.anti-bullyingalliance.org.uk

Confronting Conflict in Schools Audit. Leap Confronting Conflict, 8 Lennox Road, London, N4 3NW. +44 (0) 20 7272 5630, www.leaplinx.com/youth/schools.htm

Event Mapper: Mapping Attitudes. Curriculum, Evaluation and Management Centre, Durham University, www.cemcentre.org/RenderPage.asp?LinkID =31820000

The Hertfordshire Framework for School Self-Evaluation, www.thegrid.org.uk/leadership/sse/

Her Majesty's Inspectorate of Education (HMIE) (2002) *How Good Is Our School?* www.hmie.gov.uk/publication.asp

National Healthy School Standard. (NHSS), www.wiredforhealth.gov.uk/cat.php?catid=966&docid=7479

School Self-Evaluation, www.sheu.org.uk/survey/sse.htm

Scottish Office Education Department/Her Majesty's Inspectorate of Education (SOEID/HMIE) (1992) *Using Ethos Indicators in Primary School Self-Evaluation: Taking Account of the Views of Pupils, Parents and Teachers,* www.ethosnet.co.uk

School Emotional Environment for Learning Survey (SEELS), www.antidote. org.uk/offer/seels.html

Varnava, G. (2005) *Checkpoints for Schools: Towards a Non-Violent Society.* London: NSPCC. A copy of the document can be downloaded from www.nspcc.org.uk/Inform/TrainingAndConsultancy/Consultancy/ SupportingProductsAndResources/CheckpointsForSchools_asp_ifega234 28.html

Wirral Health Promoting Schools Scheme. Health Links, 49 Hamilton Square, Birkenhead, CH41 5AR. Tel: +44 (0) 151 647 0211, www.wirralhealth. org.uk/healthlinks/youth.asp

Resources: Activities

Department for Education and Skills (DfES) *Bullying: Don't suffer in Silence – An Anti-Bullying Pack for Schools,* retrieved 23 March 2006 from www. teachernet.gov.uk/wholeschool/behaviour/tacklingbullying/antibullying pack/

Laws, S. and Mann, G. (2004) *So You Want to Involve Children in Research? A Toolkit Supporting Children's Meaningful and Ethical Participation in Research Relating to Violence Against Children,* retrieved 21 October 2005 from www.unicef.ca/mission/childProtection/violencestudy.php

Masheder, M. (1997) *Let's Co-Operate.* London: Green Print.

Steiner, M. (1993) *Learning From Experience: Cooperative Learning and Global Education.* Stoke-on-Trent: Trentham Books.

UN Secretary-General's Study on Violence Against Children: North American Regional Consultation, *Focus Groups 101: A Guidebook for Facilitators,* retrieved 27 October 2005 from www.violenciastudioalc.org/ documentos/focusgroups101guidetofacilitators.pdf

Activity Handout 5.1 What Would You Do If ... ?

GROUP 1: What would you do if ...

1 A member of the working group is regularly late for meetings and the other group members are irritated?

2 In working group meetings, a member is over-enthusiastic and keeps interrupting the other members when they are speaking?

3 During data collection, in a small group interview, the participants are very silent, unresponsive and reluctant to answer your questions?

4 During data collection, part way through a small group interview, some staff members say they must leave to attend to other matters?

5 On the final day of the needs analysis, important new information arises which contradicts an earlier key finding?

6 In the meeting to discuss the choice of intervention, the head teacher tries to influence the decision?

GROUP 2: What would you do if ...

1 During working group meetings one member frequently gives negative criticism during group discussions?

2 One of the working group members keeps missing the meetings?

3 In front of a group of young people, one member of the working group contradicts what one of the young people has just said?

4 The head teacher wishes to conduct the interviews during the data collection process, but you fear that he/she will intimidate the participants?

5 A parent calls you over to discuss the needs analysis as you are walking to your car at the end of the day looking forward to getting home?

6 You realize towards the end of the needs analysis that very few pupils have been interviewed to find out their views?

7 During the needs analysis, the majority of people in the school identify conflict resolution and conflict management as more important than the work that your school is currently focusing on?

GROUP 3: What would you do if ...

1 After the initial briefing of your working group, during which members appeared to have a good grasp of the concepts and objectives of the needs analysis, they do not seem to know how to begin?

2 One of the working group members accuses another of making an offensive remark and refuses to work with that person?

3 During data collection, the information on behaviour management received from the pupils largely contradicts that collected from the teaching staff?

4 One working group member is not participating in the group discussions, during which the information collected is being analysed and a

continued overleaf

—continued from previous page—

set of shared goals is being formulated?

5 A parent who has accompanied the working group on one of their data consultation exercises, misrepresents the purpose of the needs analysis to other parents?

6 After the needs analysis has been completed you meet a governor who knows a lot about emotional literacy but you have already formulated your action plan?

GROUP 4: What would you do if ...

1 During a working group meeting you find that a set of shared goals has been designed by a breakaway group without consulting other members?

2 During working group meetings, one member is taking a condescending and patronizing attitude towards the pupil representatives and tends to lecture rather than to listen?

3 During a brainstorming exercise with parents, the more articulate and smarter dressed parents dominate the discussions about behaviour management?

4 During data collection, you have asked a group of young people to discuss behaviour management in the school but they do not seem to know how to begin?

5 You arrive at school having planned to conduct some focus groups, but the working group is nervous and unsure how to start?

6 The information you collect from the staff seems to contradict that collected from the head teacher?

(Adapted from Pretty et al., 1995)

6 | Children helping children through peer support

Objectives

- To understand the role that young people play in helping one another through peer support in the school community.
- To be familiar with the skills involved in training peer supporters in school.

What Is Peer Support?

This chapter introduces you to peer support – what it looks like, its benefits, and how you can train pupils and staff to implement it. Peer support describes a range of activities and systems within which people's potential to be helpful to one another can be fostered through appropriate training. Around 50 per cent of primary and secondary schools in the UK now use it as part of their anti-bullying policy. The Children's Commissioner (Aynsley-Green, 2006) strongly advocates peer support as an effective intervention against bullying.

There are four key aspects of peer support:

- Selected peers are trained to be peer supporters. An immediate aim here is to give peer supporters certain skills, often including opportunities to learn good communication skills, to share information and to reflect on their achievements; to develop perspective-taking and empathic abilities; and to deal with interpersonal conflicts, social exclusion, violence and bullying in proactive and non-violent ways.
- Certain peers will be users of the peer support scheme(s). The aim here is that they will be helped in this way, either directly by the peer supporter, or by the peer supporter arranging or encouraging other forms of help.
- A longer-term aim of such schemes is to improve peer relationships generally and to reduce rates of unresolved conflicts and bullying among pupils in the school.

- At the broadest level, the existence of a peer support scheme raises the profile of the school as a caring institution. We know that it leads to greater enjoyment of school and break times, and increased feelings of safety in school.

Essential skills of peer support include:

- good communication;
- active listening;
- empathy for a peer's distress;
- respect for something told in confidence;
- knowledge of the boundaries of confidentiality;
- an attitude of tolerance and respect;
- ability to accept constructive feedback on your capacity to help;
- willingness to adopt a problem-solving stance;
- openness to new ideas.

Case Study 6.1 What can the bystander do?

Drama is an extremely effective way of training pupils in the skills of peer support. Since the participants are in role, they are free to discuss issues that might be embarrassing if they refer directly to an individual's real-life experience. Drama also offers young people opportunities to practise a range of ways of responding to a violent incident and to explore how each person in the scenario may be feeling. Drama also offers training in knowing when it is not appropriate to intervene – or when it may be too dangerous. In this scenario, devised by trainers from ABC Training and Support, Steve Wooldridge and Jill Knell (abcservices.org.uk) – three girls, in the presence of an audience of fellow peer supporters, enact an everyday situation in which a peer supporter can try out a number of interventions to help a pupil who is being bullied in the corridor during break time.

The incident

Gemma and Nicky are saying nasty things about everyone who passes by. They make rude comments about what people are wearing and deride their appearance. Anne, who is new to the school, approaches them and timidly asks the way to the sixth-form block where she is meeting her sister, Stephanie. Gemma and Nicky burst out laughing, mimic the way Anne speaks and repeat the words 'sister' and 'Stephanie' with exaggerated lisps. They then give Anne vague directions and block her way as she tries to move on past them. Anne reacts fearfully and clearly does not know what to do next. She retreats in a dejected way.

Freeze

At this point, the trainer asks the audience of peer supporters to suggest some options for action on the part of a peer supporter who would like to

continued opposite

Case Study 6.1 continued

intervene. The scenario is re-enacted with each of the options and the audience and the role-players are invited to discuss their feelings and perceptions.

Option 1: Confront the bullies

Sarah, a peer supporter, confronts Nicky and Gemma publicly. They in turn become very aggressive and tell her loudly to mind her own business. The confrontation is now being observed by a growing number of bystanders. The audience and the role-players discuss the outcome. Anne reports that she feels humiliated and disempowered. The audience conclude that Sarah has unwittingly escalated the situation and made a private matter public. She has also failed to show empathy for Anne's feelings. Anne may well be targeted again by Gemma and Nicky.

Option 2: Offer immediate help to the pupil who is being bullied

Katie, another peer supporter, intervenes to help Anne by offering to take her personally to the sixth-form block. Gemma and Nicky jeer angrily as Katie leads Anne away. As before, a number of bystanders gather round to watch. The audience and role-players discuss the outcome. The advantage of this intervention is that it takes Anne out of a difficult situation but at the same time it makes Anne look weak and ineffectual. Gemma and Nicky have become angry and so may pick on Anne the next time they see her. Katie, like Sarah, has brought unwelcome attention to Anne and may make life worse for her. Again, the intention was good but the outcome may not be successful.

Option 3: Offer help in private to the pupil who is being bullied

Nimmi, another peer supporter, waits until Anne is on her own, as she retreats away from Gemma and Nicky. Nimmi accompanies her to the sixth-form block and helps her to find her sister. On the way, she checks that Anne is all right, shows empathy for what she has just experienced and finds out what Anne herself would find most helpful as she settles into her new school. Nimmi has information on clubs and lunchtime activities that Anne may find interesting. She has also demonstrated her sensitivity to Anne's feelings and has shown respect for her privacy by talking to her in confidence away from public view. The audience and role-players discuss this outcome and conclude that this is the best of the three options for all involved.

Types of Peer Support

The systems of peer support vary quite widely across schools and according to the age groups of the peer supporters themselves. However, its most common forms involve the following:

- *being a buddy or befriender* – for example, helping bullied peers or looking out for pupils that are isolated or excluded at break times;

- *running a lunchtime club* – for example, a club for peers who may be finding it hard to make friends;
- *conflict resolution* – mediating between peers who are in dispute;
- *mentoring* – for example, running induction sessions for new pupils;
- *one-to-one support* – giving confidential help to an individual pupil with particular interpersonal difficulties;
- *developing information services* – for example, creating lists of useful web-sites on such topics as bullying;
- *email support* – offering cyber-chatrooms for confidential support.

Benefits to Peer Supporters

Peer Supporters

Peer supporters usually report that they benefit from the helping process, that they feel more confident in themselves and that they learn to value other people more. The most frequently mentioned benefits are:

- an increase in self-confidence;
- a sense of responsibility through making school a safer place to be;
- a belief that they are contributing positively to the life of the school community;
- developing communication skills such as active listening;
- becoming skilled at making changes to the peer systems as they evolve over time.

There are also useful links with other systems, such as external training agencies (for example, ChildLine), and higher education (for example, a university-based research project), each of which offers potential for wider dissemination of the work of the peer supporters, for example, through presentations at conferences, publication of achievements in newsletters, and opportunities to meet and learn from peer supporters from other schools.

Users of Peer Support Systems

For vulnerable pupils, use of the peer support system can be a critical part of the process of feeling more positive about themselves in dealing with difficulties such as victimization or social exclusion. They report that:

- the service provides someone who listens;
- users are helped to overcome the problem themselves;
- the existence of the peer support system indicates that the school cares about their well-being.

Peer Relationships

Teachers report that the school environment becomes more caring following the introduction of a peer support scheme, and that peer relationships in general improve. They report that the presence of a peer support system:

- reduces the negative impact of bullying on victims;
- makes it more acceptable for them to report bullying, especially as peers are able to detect bullying at a much earlier stage than adults;
- enables pupils to resolve situations by themselves in a peaceful way;
- enables vulnerable pupils to be spotted more easily, in part due to the increased awareness of pupils;
- enhances the reputation of the school in the local community.

The degree to which the school integrates peer support into the whole-school policy and the school development plan is essential for its success. Schools must make pupils aware of the scheme, through the use of assemblies, newsletters, posters and presentations. The active support of the head teacher or a senior leadership figure is a crucial factor. Their role is to:

- provide time and resources for dedicated scheme coordinators to undertake the day-to-day overseeing of the programme;
- support continued training for the peer supporters, thus reducing the pressure and responsibilities placed on them;
- ensure that the scheme is integrated into the whole-school anti-bullying policy.

Case Study 6.2 Using email to provide a confidential peer support service

An all boys' school wanted to involve the pupils in decision-making after an incident of physical bullying. To this end, the school ran focus groups with all Year 9 boys, asking them to identify any gaps in the school's pastoral care system. One of the services requested by the pupils was an email peer support scheme on the grounds that it allowed counselling anonymity and confidentiality to those seeking help. Eighty-two boys volunteered to be peer supporters on day one of the recruitment drive. The volunteers were whittled down to 25 through a process of peer-selection, based on their responses to a standardized application form. Volunteers were wide-ranging – some had experienced being bullied, others had witnessed it as bystanders. A teacher mediated the email scheme to ensure anonymity, and to maintain supervision of the more serious cases. Boys seeking peer support were required to use their school email account (which they could access remotely through the web from home) to a generic email address. A teacher, who cut and pasted the text onto a blank page and then forwarded it on to the peer supporters, logged incoming emails. The peer supporters responded in their groups of four and returned their

continued overleaf

┌─ *continued from previous page* ──────────────────────────┐

response to the teacher, who then sent it on to the correct email account. The
email peer supporters were able to give helpful guidance to peers on such
topics as: being isolated; falling out with a close friend; finding it difficult to get
any positive feedback from one particular teacher; wondering whether to fight
back when being picked on or whether to use other strategies.

└──┘

Source: Hutson and Cowie (in press)

Activities for the Training Event

For a number of more detailed peer support training activities, please refer
to Cowie and Jennifer et al. (2007) which you can download freely from the
website www.vista-europe.org.

Activity 6.1 Think of a Secret (25 minutes)

Purpose
- To identify the qualities of the good peer supporter.
- To provide the opportunity to recognize that the people on the training
  course already possess many of these qualities.

Materials
  Flip chart and pens.

Procedure
Ask each person in the group to think of a secret that they have never told
anyone and/or something they would find it very hard to talk about.
*Emphasize that they will not be asked to reveal this secret at any time in the activ-
ity.* Then ask them to look around the group and think about which person
in the group they would tell their secret to if they had to tell one person.
Ask them not to reveal who this person is. Now ask them what it is about that
person that made them choose him or her.

Discussion
Take feedback from the group by asking them to call out the attributes of
the people they have chosen. Write this in a list that can be seen by the
group and that will be 'kept for future reference'. When the list is complete,
ask the group to provide a title. Usually they will see that it should be called
something like 'The Qualities of a Peer Supporter'. Finally draw attention to
the fact that they already had these qualities within the group. This sets the
group up on the positive note that they have skills to learn but that they
already possess some of the basic qualities needed.

Activity 6.2 Reflection (20 minutes)

Purpose
- To identify actions that are helpful and those that are not.
- To build on the qualities already identified in Activity 6.1.

Materials
   None.

Procedure
Ask participants to think individually about a time when they turned to someone for help when they were being bullied or treated badly. What did that helpful person do? How did it feel to be helped? What was useful? What was unhelpful? Ask each person to make two columns on a piece of paper. One heading is 'Peer supporters do … '. The other is 'Peer supporters do not … '. *Emphasize that they will not be asked to reveal their issue at any time in the activity.*

Discussion
In the plenary, the facilitator summarizes responses in the same two columns on a flip chart. The facilitator then invites the group to reflect on how they can encourage pupils to act in supportive ways at all times towards one another and how to make them aware of unhelpful behaviour.

Activity 6.3 Roadblocks to Communication (25 minutes)

Purpose
- To illustrate the importance of attending by providing the opportunity to feel what it is like not to be attended to.
- To illustrate the importance of listening by providing the opportunity to feel what it is like not to be listened to.

Materials
   Activity Handout 6.1 Behaviour Cards

Procedure
Ask people to get into pairs – one is invited to act as a 'peer supporter', the other as a 'supportee' – and sit on their chairs facing each other. Ask the supportee to think of a problem (nothing serious) they could talk about. Give the peer supporter a card (Activity Handout 6.1 Behaviour Cards) with instructions on how to behave and ask them to do exactly what the card says. Half of the peer supporters adopt response 6.1.1; the other half adopt response 6.1.2.

Discussion
After just three minutes, stop the action and bring the group back together.

Feedback should be taken first from the supportee as to how it felt to be ignored or talked over. This activity usually provokes strong feelings of anger on not being valued, in addition to much laughter. Then take feedback from the peer supporters about how it felt to behave in this unhelpful way. We usually conclude with a question to the group about what they think we want them to take from this activity. This conclusion need not be complex or sophisticated but it is important to summarize in order to ensure that everyone has got the point you intended and remembers it when they are using their peer support skills in a real situation. Finally, participants return to their pairs and replay the role play, only this time the peer supporters demonstrate active listening skills using response 6.1.3.

Activity 6.4 To Advise or Not to Advise (40 minutes)

Purpose
- To provide an opportunity to practise responding to a direct request for advice.
- To begin to practise helping someone without advising them.

Materials
> Activity Handout 6.2 Role Card for Supportee.
> Activity Handout 6.3 Observer's Checklist.

Procedure
Divide the group into smaller groups of three and assign or ask for volunteers for three roles for a role play – *peer supporter, supportee* and *observer*. Give the supportee a role card (Activity Handout 6.2 Role Card for Supportee) with a storyline including a problem on it. It should take only a few minutes for them to tell their story to the peer supporter. Instruct them to ask the peer supporter directly what he or she thinks they should do about their problem once they have told their story. If the peer supporter avoids the question, suggest that they ask it again more forcefully. The peer supporter should not be told the exact purpose of the activity. Instruct the peer supporter simply to do what they can to help the supportee. Tell the observer the purpose of the activity and ask them to record what the peer supporter does and says in response to the question, using Activity Handout 6.3 Observer's Checklist, p. 80

Discussion
When the role play is over, the observer should give feedback to the peer supporter regarding how they responded and the effect of that response on the supportee. In the large group, there can be further discussion of how best to respond to the pressure of someone wanting advice. The small groups reconvene and replay the same encounter, only this time the peer supporter uses active listening skills.

Activity 6.5 Reflections on Peer Support (40 minutes)

Purpose
- To increase participants' awareness of the range of responses that exists within the group.
- To make connections among the responses.
- To reflect on the learning that has taken place during the session.

Materials
    The flip chart, The Qualities of the Peer Supporter, created from participants' responses to Activity 6.1, Think of a Secret.

Procedure
The facilitators invite the group to consider the range of responses that they have offered or experienced during the session. What feelings do they experience when they are offering help to another person? What feelings do they experience when they are offered support? Participants are invited to write their responses on a piece of paper. After 10 minutes (or when everyone has finished), participants are asked to read their comments aloud one by one. Then comments are invited from the rest of the group.

Discussion (it may be helpful to return to the two columns created by the group for Activity 6.2)
This is an opportunity to share patterns in the ways in which the group offers and receives peer support, for example, because of gender or ethnicity or age. Explore what are the most common themes and those that are least common. Does anyone in the group find it hard to receive peer support? Why? How frequently do individuals in the group experience support from others? Could peer support be enhanced in their own work environments? What will each person take away with them from this session?

Further Reading

Aynsley-Green, A. (2006) *Bullying Today*. Office of the Children's Commissioner, www.childrenscommissioner.org/documents/bullying%20today%20(november%202006).pdf

Cowie, H. and Hutson, N. (2005) 'Peer support: a strategy to help bystanders challenge school bullying', *Pastoral Care in Education*, 23(22): 40–4.

Hutson, H. and Cowie, H. (in press) 'Setting up an email peer support service', *Pastoral Care in Education*.

Websites

ABC Training and Support, www.abcservices.org.uk

ChildLine, www.childline.org.uk/

Cowie, H. and Jennifer, D. et al. (2007) *School Bullying and Violence: Taking Action*, www.vista-europe.org

Scherer-Thompson, J. (2002) *Peer Support Manual*. London: Mental Health Foundation, UK Office, 83 Victoria Street, London SW1H 0HW, www.mentalhealth.org.uk/

Sky High Peer Support and Mentoring Training, www.sky-high.org.uk/

UK Observatory for the Promotion of Non-violence, www.ukobservatory.com

National Society for the Prevention of Cruelty to Children (NSPCC), www.nspcc.org.uk/asp/SSSearch.asp

Resources

Cole, T. (2000) *Kids helping kids*. Victoria, BC: Peer Resources.

Cowie, H. and Wallace, P. (2000) *Peer Support in Action*. London: Sage Publications.

Department for Education and Employment (2000) *Bullying: Don't Suffer in Silence: An Anti-bullying Pack for Schools*, 2nd edn. London: HMSO.

Petch, B. and Withers, T. (2006) *Peer Mediation: Guidance Notes for Schools*. Solihull Metropolitan Borough Council, PO Box 20, Council House, Solihull, West Midlands B91 3QU, UK.

Salter, K. and Twidle, R. (2005) *The Learning Mentor's Source and Resource Book*. London: Paul Chapman Publishing.

Evaluations

Cowie, H. (1998) 'Perspective of teachers and pupils on the experience of peer support against bullying', *Educational Research and Evaluation*, 4: 108–25.

Cunningham, C., Cunningham, L., Martorelli, V., Tran, A., Young, J. and Zacharias, R. (1998) 'The effects of primary division, student-mediated conflict resolution programs on playground aggression', *Journal of Child Psychology and Psychiatry*, 39: 653–62.

Menesini, E., Codecasa, E., Benelli, B. and Cowie, H. (2003) 'Enhancing children's responsibility to take action against bullying: evaluation of a befriending intervention in Italian middle schools', *Aggressive Behavior*, 29: 1–14.

Mental Health Foundation (2002) *Peer support: Someone to turn to. An evaluation report of the Mental Health Foundation Peer Support Programme.*

London and Glasgow: Mental Health Foundation.

Naylor, P. and Cowie, H. (1999) 'The effectiveness of peer support systems in challenging school bullying: the perspectives and experiences of teachers and pupils', *Journal of Adolescence*, 22: 467–79.

Smith, P.K. and Watson, D. (2004) *Evaluation of the CHIPS (ChildLine in Partnership with Schools) programme*. Research report RR570, DfES publications, PO Box 5050, Sherwood Park, Annesley, Nottingham NG15 0DJ.

Stacey, H. (2000) 'Mediation and peer mediation', in H. Cowie and P. Wallace, *Peer Support in Action*. London: Sage Publications. pp. 23–35.

Activity Handout 6.1 Behaviour Cards

Response 6.1.1 When your partner starts to talk, look at the floor or off into the distance, shift in your seat, clean your nails, generally look bored. Do not offer any response that encourages the person to carry on talking, just say, 'Yeah, Yeah' in a bored way.

Response 6.1.2 As soon as your partner has described their dilemma, interrupt, talking over them if necessary to give advice. Tell them how you would handle the situation. Don't leave much space for your partner to talk about their experience. Say something like, 'You think that's bad? You should hear what happened to me!'

Response 6.1.3 As your partner talks, keep eye contact, nod sympathetically, speak very little but indicate your attentiveness though such comments as, 'Mmm', 'I understand', 'I wonder how you felt then ... ' and 'I appreciated it that you shared this with me ... '.

Activity Handout 6.2 Role Card for Supportee

I had a big argument with my best friend, Jay, three weeks ago. Since then, Jay has not spoken to me at all. Not only that, Jay has got everyone else in the class to ignore me and leave me out. So I spend all my time alone. I have never felt so bad in my life. Tell me what I should do. Note to supportee. Whatever the peer supporter says, keep asking such questions as, 'Yes but what do you think I should do?' or 'Tell me exactly what to do.' or 'What would you do if you were in my situation?' or 'You keep on agreeing with me but I want some advice on what to do.'

Activity Handout 6.3 Observer's Checklist

Your task is to observe the quality of the interaction between peer supporter and supportee. Look particularly at the following: eye contact; gestures; body position; facial expression; tone of voice. Write general comments about the way the peer supporter responded to the supportee.

- **What messages were conveyed by the peer supporter's eyes, gestures, body position, facial expression?**

  _____

  _____

  _____

  _____

  _____

  _____

- **How appropriate was the voice of the peer supporter?**

  _____

  _____

  _____

  _____

  _____

  _____

- **How interested did the peer supporter appear in the supportee's problem?**

  _____

  _____

  _____

  _____

  _____

  _____

Provide evidence for each of your comments

7 | Emotional literacy in schools

Objectives

- To raise awareness of the importance of emotional literacy.
- To become familiar with some of the skills involved in providing opportunities for the development of emotional literacy.

Overview

Many educators and academics across Europe are rejecting the view that academic achievement is the sole goal towards which children and young people should work if they want to be well educated and successful. Instead, there is a growing recognition that teaching emotional literacy is as equally important to children and young people's development as the academic curriculum. Increasing levels of dissatisfaction with school (by children, young people and adults alike), rising levels of interpersonal violence, a lowering of the age at which such violence is noted, and stagnation in the progress of academic improvement as measured by school-based and external testing are cited as evidence for this. Thus, in the UK, the Department of Health (DoH, 2004) published *Promoting Emotional Health and Well-Being Through the National Healthy School Standard*, which reinforced the need to consider the development of non-academic aspects of school life. At the same time, the Department for Education and Skills (DfES, 2004) released *Every Child Matters: Change for Children in Schools*, a report which identified five outcomes for all children: be healthy; stay safe; enjoy and achieve; make a positive contribution; and achieve economic well-being. All five outcomes require strong emotional foundations. In the UK, the DfES has acknowledged the importance of a taught curriculum designed to develop young people's emotional capacity, with its recent development of its Social and Emotional Aspects of Learning (SEAL) programme.

What Is Emotional Literacy?

The leading research on the concept of emotional intelligence originated with Salovey and Mayer in the late 1980s (Salovey and Mayer, 1990), whose definition included the concept of growth as well as understanding. They suggested that emotional intelligence involves the ability to 'perceive emotions, access and generate emotions so as to facilitate thought, to understand emotions and emotional knowledge, and to reflectively regulate emotions so as to promote emotional and intellectual growth' (Mayer and Salovey, 1997: 5). In his book, *Emotional Intelligence: Why It Can Matter More Than IQ*, Goleman (1996) popularized the concept of emotional intelligence and introduced the notion that it should be regarded as the strongest indicator of human success. He used powerful arguments to demonstrate that personal success, academic achievement and even better health can be achieved through the development of emotional as well as intellectual capacity. If Salovey and Mayer's and Goleman's views, and the acknowledgements implicit in the DoH and DfES documentation are accepted, what can schools do to support the development of emotional intelligence?

We believe that the means of achieving emotional intelligence and its associated growth is through the development of emotional literacy. While a wide variety of definitions are documented, Weare (2004: 2) defines emotional literacy as the

> Ability to understand ourselves and other people, and in particular to be aware of, understand, and use information about the emotional states of ourselves and others with competence. It includes the ability to understand, express and manage our own emotions, and respond to the emotions of others, in ways that are helpful to ourselves and others.

More importantly, however, in promoting a whole-school community approach to the promotion of non-violence, we note the research evidence that suggests that: 'the school environment is the largest determinant of the level of emotional and social competence and well-being in pupils and teachers' (Weare and Grey, 2003). Thus, we find Weare's (2004: 2) definition of the emotional literate community very useful. She defines the emotional literacy in an organization as 'the extent to which the organization takes into account the role of emotion in dealing with the people who are its members, and in planning, making and implementing decisions, and takes positive steps to promote the emotional and social well-being of its members' (Weare, 2004: 2).

Taken together, these definitions draw attention to the interrelationship between the individual and his or her environment, which suggests the idea that an individual's ability to behave in an emotionally literate fashion will be affected by both the quality of his or her interpersonal relationships with others, and the overall social context.

Indeed, in their development of the *School Emotional Environment for Learning Survey* instrument, Haddon et al.'s (2005) research suggested that the experience of emotional literacy was strongly affected by a number of factors, including:

- the quality of relationships an individual has with others at school – between pupils, between pupils and staff, between staff colleagues and between staff and management;
- how effectively individuals communicated with each other, both formally and informally;
- the extent to which the individuals felt supported by the organization's structures and systems.

Examples of Social and Emotional Competencies

Emotional literacy is concerned with a number of social and emotional competencies that may be useful to some individuals some of the time.

- Self-understanding:
  - holding an accurate and positive view of ourselves;
  - having a sense of optimism about ourselves and the world;
  - having a coherent and continuous life story.
- Understanding and managing emotions:
  - experiencing the whole range of emotions;
  - understanding the causes of our emotions;
  - expressing our emotions appropriately;
  - managing our responses to our emotions effectively (for example, managing anger, controlling impulses);
  - knowing how to feel good more often and for longer;
  - using emotion information to plan and solve problems;
  - resilience, that is, processing and recovering from difficult emotional experiences.
- Understanding social situations and forming relationships:
  - forming attachments with other people;
  - experiencing empathy for others;
  - communicating and responding effectively with others;
  - managing relationships effectively;
  - being autonomous, that is, independent and self-reliant (Weare, 2004).

Benefits of an Emotionally Literate School

There is strong evidence regarding work on emotional literacy that suggests a wide range of educational and social benefits, including:

- improved behaviour;

- improved academic standards;
- increased inclusion;
- improved relationships among pupils, staff and parents;
- an ethos of respect for others;
- improved working and learning environment for all members of the school community;
- improved emotional and mental health for all members of the school community;
- engagement in activities that promote emotional health and well-being, making it less likely that young people will engage in negative activities such as use and abuse of alcohol and drugs, missing school, engaging in bullying and aggressive behaviour (Antidote, 2003).

More specifically, for schools that make a commitment to developing the emotional literacy skills of their young people, Sharpe (2001) suggests that the following outcomes will be achieved:

- Children will recognize and understand their feelings, and will become more adept at handling and expressing them appropriately.
- Children and teachers will become less stressed, and will be able to manage competing demands more effectively.
- Children will become better listeners, and will be more likely to appreciate others' points of view.
- Children will experience an increase in attention span.
- Children will experience greater proficiency at forming and maintaining relationships.
- Children will learn problem-solving methods that lead to enhanced interpersonal skills as adults.
- Children will learn to manage conflicts, with less likelihood that they will become involved in crime, particularly those crimes involving violence.
- Children will learn skills that will enhance their future parenting skills.

Not only does emotional literacy enhance learning and well-being in a school community, it fosters open communication among all members of the organization, it enables young people and staff to find their own solutions to problems, and it encourages staff and pupils to reflect on their relationships with each other. Nevertheless, developing emotional literacy in your school does not offer a 'quick fix' for the promotion of non-violence. Rather, it represents an ongoing process of engaging with others and seeking to understand others' emotions. Furthermore, individual capacity to practise emotional literacy varies according to the organizational and social context within which it takes place. Case Study 7.1 provides an example of how implementing an emotional literacy curriculum programme has the potential to reduce school violence.

Case Study 7.1 *Second Step: A Violence Prevention Curriculum*

An example of a programme specifically designed to reduce impulsive and aggressive behaviour in children and young people by increasing their emotional and social competency skills is *Second Step*, published by the Committee for Children (2002).

Second Step consists of commercially available curriculum materials, a family guide, learning materials and training for educators. Based on techniques developed by cognitive behaviour therapists, the programme offers a class-based programme for use with nursery school children through to Year 10, that teaches children to change attitudes and behaviours that contribute to violence. Using suggested lesson scripts, each with clear objectives and preparatory activities, teachers introduce key concepts through class discussion stimulated by photo cards or video taped stories.

The programme consists of thirty 35-minute lessons or fifteen 50-minute lessons (depending on age) during which children and young people learn to practise pro-social behaviour. Lessons involve group discussion, role play, modelling, coaching and practise to increase pupils' proficiency in social competency, risk assessment, decision-making, self-regulation and positive goal-setting. The programme's lesson content focuses on empathy (the identification and understanding of one's own emotions and those of others), impulse control and problem-solving (choosing positive goals, reducing impulsiveness, evaluating the consequences of behaviour in terms of safety, fairness and impact on others), and anger management (managing emotional reactions, engaging in decision-making when highly aroused).

A number of evaluation studies have been carried out on the *Second Step* programme. Observational studies of elementary school children in their classrooms, dining rooms and on the playground have found decreased levels of physical aggression and increased levels of pro-social behaviour in pupils who have received the programme (Grossman et al., 1997). More recently, Frey et al. (2005) found that, when compared with children from control groups, pupils who had received *Second Step* were more likely to prefer pro-social goals, require less adult intervention for minor conflicts, behave less aggressively and, among girls, behave more cooperatively. Research to evaluate *Second Step*, Grades 4–5 version, revealed that adolescents were less tolerant of physical aggression, verbal aggression and social exclusion than control participants were, and less likely to view pro-social skills as difficult to perform (Van Schoiack Edstrom et al., 2002). Interestingly, Grossman et al.'s (1997) observations showed that in control schools that did not receive the *Second Step* programme, pupil behaviour had deteriorated, with increased physical and verbal aggression at six month follow-up. This suggests that the potential for such an intervention to promote non-violence is more significant than at first appears.

Taken together, the results of these studies indicate that *Second Step* has a positive effect on pupil behaviour in school, promoting socially responsible behaviour and discouraging aggressive behaviour. The evidence supports the idea that interventions that focus on emotional and social competencies and the development of pro-social skills have important implications for the reduction

continued overleaf

> **Case Study 7.1** continued
>
> and prevention of bullying and aggressive behaviour. This intervention is part of
> a wider movement to promote emotional literacy by enabling individuals to find
> ways of managing their emotions, feeling socially connected to each other, and
> engaging in activities that promote both physical and emotional well-being.
> Other such interventions include Miss Dorothy, Promoting Alternative Thinking
> Strategies (PATHS), The Incredible Years and *The Box Full of Feelings* (see
> Websites, Emotional Literacy Interventions and Evaluations, Resources sections
> for further details).

Activities for the Training Event

Activity 7.1 Identifying Emotions (30 minutes) (adapted from Cowie and Wallace, 2000)

Purpose
- To encourage participants to identify and own their individual emotions.

Materials
  None.

Procedure
Divide the large group into pairs. In pairs, participants decide which one
will be A, the identifier, and which one will be B, the listener. A is given a
set of unfinished sentences to complete, each describing how a person feels
in a range of different contexts, for example: 'When people are nice to me,
I feel … '. After each sentence, B paraphrases what A said. Suggested sentences might include:

- *When no-one speaks to me, I feel …*
- *When people are nasty to me, I feel …*
- *When people put me down, I feel …*
- *When I am unappreciated, I feel …*
- *When I am excluded from the group, I feel …*
- *When I am the odd one out, I feel …*
- *When someone praises me, I feel …*

After about 10 minutes, reverse the roles so that B completes the same
unfinished sentences with A as the listener.

Discussion
With the whole group, discuss which feelings were easier to describe than
others, and explore what the implications of this are for developing emotional literacy. Discuss the range of words that can be used to paraphrase a

feeling. Encourage participants not to comment on the content of their partner's statements. This activity provides the opportunity for members of the group to explore whether some emotions are harder to talk about than others. It also provides an opportunity for participants to develop their vocabulary for talking about emotions.

Activity 7.2 Understanding Feelings (30 minutes) *(adapted from Cowie and Wallace, 2000)*

Purpose
- To give participants the opportunity to develop the skills of active listening and communicating empathy.

Materials
   None.

Procedure
Divide participants into groups of three. Ask each group to select a speaker, a listener and an observer. Give each speaker a few minutes to select a personal topic on which to speak, about which he or she feels strongly. Without interruption by the listener, the speaker talks about their chosen topic. The listener listens for the feelings behind the account. The observer watches in silence. After listening to the account, the listener summarizes what the speaker said on their chosen topic, paying attention to the speaker's feelings, and not the details of the story. Reverse the roles so that each participant has the opportunity to experience being the speaker, the listener and the observer.

Discussion
Within the groups of three, encourage participants to discuss their experience of this activity. Prompt questions might include:

- *In your role as speaker/listener/observer, how did you feel?*
- *In your role as speaker, was it helpful to have the listener summarize your words? How might it have been different?*
- *In your role as listener, was it difficult to summarize the speaker's comments? If so, why?*
- *In your role as speaker/listener/observer, did you sense any difficulties or experience any awkward moments?*
- *In your role as speaker/listener/observer, did you observe any barriers that obstructed effective listening?*

This activity promotes discussion of different feelings and perspectives in different situations. Not only does it promote the opportunity for the speaker to communicate their feelings, it also enables the listener and the observer to take the perspective of the speaker, which helps to foster empathy skills. Since each person experiences all three roles, this activity also provides scope for giving and receiving constructive feedback.

Activity 7.3 Statues (60 minutes)

Purpose
- To enable participants to gain new insights into their own and others' feelings and emotions.
- To change participants' experience of feeling unsupported by their school in a given situation.

Materials
   None.

Procedure
Ask the whole group for five volunteers to act as statues. Ask participants to think of a situation in which someone might feel unsupported by their school, class or organization (depending on whether the participants are school staff, pupils, parents and others, respectively). For example, a conflict in the playground between two 7-year-old girls, Meera and Daisy, has spilt over into the classroom at the end of playtime. Each girl is very upset and the whole class divides into two groups to support each of the girls. A student teacher, unaware of how the conflict originated, chooses to reprimand only Daisy in front of the whole class. Daisy feels that the teacher has not dealt fairly with the issue, and feels embarrassed and upset at being told off in front of all her classmates. The next day she does not want to return to school. Ask a sixth volunteer to sculpt the group of five into three scenes that represent the beginning, middle and end of the situation. Ask them to add elements of body language. Ask participants to carry out this part of the activity in complete silence. Ask another volunteer to change the scenes, however they feel is necessary, to show a better outcome for Daisy feeling supported. They can physically move the statues or take them away altogether.

Discussion
This is a very powerful exercise, for statues and observers alike, particularly as it is carried out in silence. It focuses attention on emotional experiences and reactions to one another. During discussion, prompt questions might include:

- *How did it feel to be a statue?*
- *How did it feel to observe the evolving situation?*
- *What are the essential skills for communicating and responding effectively with others?*

- *What are the essential skills for developing resilience, that is, processing and recovering from difficult emotional experiences?*
- *What are the essential requirements for adults in school to act as positive role models?*

By using their own bodies to present a visual picture of a situation, participants gain new insights into themselves and others, and gain greater insight into their own feelings and emotions.

Activity 7.4 The Magic Chair (30 minutes)

Purpose
- To offer participants the opportunity to give and receive positive affirmation.

Materials
    A 'magic' chair.

Procedure
Divide the group into subgroups of between six to eight participants. For each group, arrange the chairs so that one chair is facing a semicircle of five to seven chairs, depending on the size of the subgroup. In turn, one participant from each subgroup takes a turn at sitting in the magic chair in front of the other members of their subgroup. The only rule for this activity is that the participant in the magic chair is prohibited from talking. Participants in the magic chair will feel compelled to respond to the feedback from their colleagues and peers, especially if they are not used to receiving positive affirmation. Try and encourage them to refrain from doing so. The other participants in each subgroup give the participant in the magic chair positive feedback about their participation in the training event, or if they know them well, about their experience of them at school. Only positive feedback is allowable, and discussion among individual participants should not be entered into! Most participants in the magic chair will find it difficult to recall what was said by their colleagues, therefore, it is helpful if one member of each subgroup acts as a scribe to write down the positive affirmations for the participant in the magic chair to refer to later.

Discussion
While this activity requires no discussion, it is worth noting that it is a very positive exercise on which to end a training event.

Further Reading

Bundy, J. and Cornwell, S. (2007) *The Emotional Curriculum*. Bristol: Lucky Duck Books.

Cowie, H., Boardman, C., Dawkins, J. and Jennifer, D. (2004) *Emotional Health and Well-Being: A Practical Guide for Schools*. London: Sage Publications.

Rae, T. and Pedersen, L. (2007) *Developing Emotional Literacy with Teenage Boys*. London: Paul Chapman Publishing.

Websites

Antidote (UK), www.antidote.org.uk

The Collaborative for Academic, Social, and Emotional Learning (CASEL), www.casel.org/home/index.php

Committee for Children (USA), www.cfchildren.org

Committee for Children (UK), www.cfchildren.org.uk/

Department for Education and Skills (DfES), www.dfes.gov.uk

Department for Education and Skills materials including the Social and Emotional Aspects of Learning (SEAL), and Social, Emotional and Behaviour Skills (SEBS) materials (UK), www.teachernet.gov.uk/teachingandlearning/socialandpastoral/sebs1/seal/themes/

Department of Health, www.wiredforhealth.gov.uk/

Miss Dorothy.com (UK), www.missdorothy.com/

The Incredible Years (US), www.incredibleyears.com/

Kids EQ, www.kidseq.com

National Emotional Literacy Interest Group, www.nelig.com

Promoting Alternative Thinking Strategies (PATHS) (US), www.channing-bete.com/positiveyouth/pages/PATHS/PATHS.html

The School of Emotional Literacy, www.schoolofemotional-literacy.com

Second Step (UK), www.cfchildren.org.uk/

UK Observatory for the Promotion of Non-Violence, www.ukobservatory.com/

Interventions and Evaluations

Miss Dorothy.com is a programme developed in and used across the UK with funding from the Home Office to give children the skills needed to keep safe. Evaluations can be found at www.missdorothy.com/home.asp?id=58&t=0

PATHS, a programme developed in the USA by Mark Greenberg and Carol Kusché, is being used extensively in the USA and in the UK. It is designed to help teachers develop young people's social emotional skills.

Greenberg, M.T. and Kusché, C. (1998) 'Preventive intervention for school-aged deaf children: The PATHS curriculum', *Journal of Deaf Studies and*

Deaf Education, 3: 49–63. A summary can be found at www.casel.org/about_sel/pathsdesc.php

Greenberg, M.T., Kusché, C. and Mihalic, S.F. (1998) *Blueprints for Violence Prevention, Book Ten: Promoting Alternative Thinking Strategies (PATHS)*. Boulder, CO: Center for the Study and Prevention of Violence, www.colorado.edu/cspv/blueprints/model/programs/PATHS.html and modelprograms.samhsa.gov/template_cf.cfm?page=model&pkProgramID=24

Second Step: A Violence Prevention Curriculum is a programme developed by the Committee for Children in Seattle, Washington. It is being used extensively in the USA and Canada and in over 200 schools across the UK. Translated versions of the programme are being used in Denmark, Norway, Sweden, Germany, Slovakia, Lithuania and Japan. An evaluation can be found at www.cfchildren.org/ssf/researchf/researchdetail

Grossman, C.D., Neckerman, H.J., Koepsell, T.D., Liu, P.Y., Ashere, K., Beland, K., Frey, K. and Rivara, F.P. (1997) 'Effectiveness of a violence prevention curriculum among children in elementary school: a randomized controlled trial', *Journal of the American Medical Association*, 277: 1605–11. modelprograms.samhsa.gov/template_cf.cfm?page=model&pkProgramID=38

Orpinas, P.I., Parcel, G.S., McAlister, A. and Frankowski, R. (1995) 'Violence prevention in middle schools: a pilot evaluation', *Journal of Adolescent Health*, 17: 360–71, www.casel.org/about_sel/secondstepdesc.php

The Incredible Years are effective, research-based programmes developed by Carolyn Webster-Stratton, M.S.N., M.P.H., Ph.D., Professor and Director of the Parenting Clinic at the University of Washington. They are aimed at reducing children's aggression and behaviour problems and increasing social competence at home and at school. Evaluations can be found at www.incredibleyears.com/evaluation/ evaluation-tudies.htm and modelprograms.samhsa.gov/template_cf.cfm?page=model&pkProgramID=29

Resources

One resource designed to support the socio-emotional development of children aged 2 to 7 includes *A Box Full of Feelings* (2001) distributed by Smallwood Publishing http://www.smallwood.co.uk. Developed at the Research Centre for Experiential Education, Leuven University, the activity set is built around four basic feelings: happiness, fear, anger and sadness. The aim of the box is to help children remain or get in touch with their inner world of feelings, recognize emotions in themselves, accept them, name them and have a more differentiated awareness of them. A sequel is also available for children aged from 5 to 10 years old entitled *A House Full of Feelings and Emotions*. Published by CEGO Publishers, Leuven, Belgium, both sets are available from www.cego.ped.kuleuven.ac.be

8 | Restorative practice

Objectives

- To understand how restorative practice can help to resolve conflicts.
- To be familiar with the basic skills involved in training teachers and pupils to engage in restorative practice.

What Is Restorative Practice?

The original concept of restorative practice came from peace-keeping practices adopted by Maori, Aboriginal and Native American populations. At its core lies the concept of a caring, inclusive community. When conflicts arise – as they inevitably will – restorative practices engage the perpetrators, their victims and significant others in the commmunity in a collective process of problem-solving whose aim is *reparation* of damage, *restoration* of the quality of relationships and facilitating the *reintegration* of participants in the conflict back into the school community. The method has been successfully used in the criminal justice system and recently adapted for schools. In contrast to traditional punitive approaches to discipline, restorative practices place more emphasis on pupils themselves resolving conflicts and so in the longer term build a strong sense of community.

There are a number of key aspects of restorative practice:

- *Reparation* is not about winning or losing, blame or revenge but about fairness and justice.
- *Restoration of the relationship* is non-punitive – the perpetrator takes responsibility for the wrong and makes amends in some way. Through the process of open, direct communication between victim and perpetrator, it potentially transforms the ways in which people relate to one another.
- *Reintegration,* at the broadest level, provides an arena in which pupils, staff and parents can be part of a just process through which they learn

the consequences of violence and come to understand the impact
:ir behaviour on others.

:rison (2003), a leading advocate of the method, points out, there are
/road outcomes to aim for: *safe school communities* and *behavioural*
 _   ;e for individuals*. But there can often be tension between the two as you
can see in Case Study 8.1.

Case Study 8.1 The community or the individual?

Leroy is a very angry and aggressive Year 9 pupil who leads an antisocial gang, is
often at the centre of nasty bullying episodes and who frequently uses
threatening language and behaviour towards women teachers. At the same
time, the head teacher knows that his father has been cautioned for engaging in
domestic violence and his mother suffers from depression. If the staff focus only
on Leroy's emotional health and well-being, the school community continues to
suffer from his aggressive outbursts. If they focus on 'zero tolerance' approaches
in order to protect the school community, Leroy will be suspended from school
but will also continue to be at risk at home and in the wider community. If the
school does nothing, the problem will simply escalate for everyone. The
restorative approach, by contrast, takes Leroy and those whom he has hurt
through a process that values accountability for the harm that has occurred as
well as emotional support for all involved. As Morrison (2003: 692) summarizes
the process: 'Through restitution the harm is repaired; through resolution the
community reduces the risk of the harm recurring; and through reconciliation
comes emotional healing.'

Schools that put a restorative philosophy into practice typically use a
range of methods that include peer mediation, adult mediation and conferencing. Strategies address violent incidents once they have occurred as
well as interventions to reduce violence. However, if the school is to make
real changes it also needs to attend to the prevention of violence in the first
place. In order to do this, restorative practice needs to be embedded into
the culture of the school in all aspects. Figure 8.1, based on Wachtel and
McCold (2001), conceptualizes a framework of a just and fair culture
grounded in positive, caring relationships.

In Figure 8.1, the vertical axis refers to the boundaries necessary to maintain good order in the whole-school community while the horizontal axis
refers to the nurture and emotional support that the community and the
individuals within it need.

- Practice which lacks structure and support is seen as *neglectful* (not engaging with people at any level when violence occurs).
- Practice which is high in control and low on support is *punitive* (exerting
  power over people by blaming participants in violence and so perpetuat-
  ing a culture of blame and stigma).

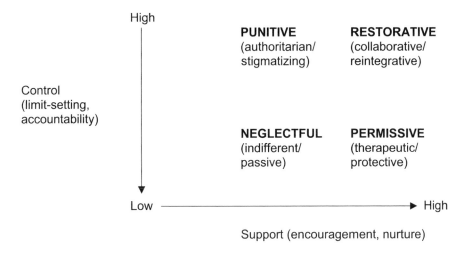

Figure 8.1 Building a framework for restorative practice

- Practice which is low on control and high on support is experienced as *permissive* (doing things *for* people but at the same time disempowering them and not challenging them so that they do not learn to be proactive in challenging violence).
- Practice which maintains high standards of behaviour and boundaries at the same time as well as being supportive is experienced as *restorative* (here the school works *with* people and so creates a culture of cooperation and facilitates a sense of responsibility and ownership of the community).

There are a number of forms of restorative practice. Here we present two that are widely used in schools to illustrate the process: *mediation* and *conferencing*. Please note that where disputes are serious and long-standing, it is essential to call in a person trained and experienced in conferencing and mediation. In this chapter, we indicate some basic techniques.

Mediation

In cases of conflict between pupils, a trained peer mediator helps the parties involved in the dispute to agree about what happened, who was harmed and about what can be done to repair the damage. The parties involved agree to make amends in some way acceptable to each one and agree to move on. The process usually takes place in a certain order. In Table 8.1 we have adopted the five steps in the mediation process recommended by Cole (2000).

Table 8.1 The five steps of mediation

Step 1 Identify the problem
Make the disputants feel comfortable. Explain what the process of mediation entails. Invite each participant to describe their view of the problem situation without interruption, stating feelings as well as facts. The facilitator clarifies the needs and interests of each party, using statements like, 'My understanding of what you said is this … '. Each party is asked to summarize what the other said.
The facilitator summarizes what each has said.

Step 2 Explore options
Each party states what ideally they would like to happen and is invited to suggest possible solutions. The facilitator notes possible risks and benefits.

Step 3 Take account of risks and benefits
The facilitator invites each party to think about the outcomes of the suggested solutions. Each is invited to explore possible risks and possible benefits of the proposed solutions.

Step 4 Make a plan of action
Each party considers which solutions are likely to meet the needs of both. They are asked to select one or two possible solutions. The facilitator clarifies what each party agrees to do and by when. The facilitator then draws up a written agreement of future actions which is signed by all present. Both parties shake hands.

Step 5 Review and evaluate
The parties agree to meet to review outcomes and to evaluate what happened. They agree to renegotiate as appropriate. The facilitator praises each party for successes and summarizes in context the values of cooperation and trust. The facilitator closes the meeting by acknowledging that progress has been made (even if complete resolution has not been reached). Each person is invited to reflect on how they might each behave differently in the future.

In Case Study 8.2, we see how peer mediators can use these five steps to help two friends who had fallen out over a boyfriend.

Case Study 8.2 Kate and Nicky quarrel over Tony

Kate and Nicky, now in Year 9, have been best friends since Year 7. They both love dancing and often meet after school to practise. They also share the same sense of humour. Two weeks ago Tony, a boy that Kate has fancied for some time, asked her out and she couldn't wait to share the news with Nicky who, at the time, seemed to be happy for her. She has been out with him once since then but he scarcely seems to notice her at school. That has made her very moody and she doubts whether he really likes her. On Monday Kate saw Nicky and Tony joking and laughing in the lunch queue. As she put it later, she could not believe that Nicky could betray her in this way. She confronted her at break and a terrible argument broke out. She accused Nicky of flirting with Tony and deliberately trying to steal her boyfriend. The argument got so intense that it nearly came to blows. The Year Head saw what was going on and suggested to the two girls that they take their issue to the school peer mediation team. They agreed to do this and the mediation took place the next day.

continued opposite

Case Study 8.2 continued

The mediators took Kate and Nicky through the five steps (see Table 8.1), as they had been trained to do.

Step 1 After making the girls comfortable, the mediators asked each to tell her side of the story. Kate told how upset she had been to see Nicky laughing with Tony when she was unable to catch his attention during school. She also told how much she had been crying over him at home and how disappointed she had been in her relationship with him. She said that when she saw them laughing together, she felt like killing Nicky and that's why she shouted at her. Nicky told how Tony was fun to be with and that she had just been joking with him in a friendly way. She actually had no idea that Kate was watching and, even if she had known, she did not think that she was doing anything wrong. She admitted that she found him attractive, as most of the girls did, but that she had no intention of taking him away from her best friend. She had been distraught when Kate shouted at her in public at break time and had only shouted back to defend herself as she was sure that Kate was going to hit her.

Step 2 The peer mediators invited the two girls in turn to say what ideally they would like to happen next. Kate said that she would like it if they could go back to being best friends as they were before. Ideally she would like to have Nicky as her best friend and Tony as her boyfriend. Nicky said that she would like the quarrel to be forgotten and to go back to how they were before. In an ideal world they could both be friends with Tony and not be jealous. Kate suggested that one solution would be for Nicky to stop talking to Tony. Nicky suggested that one solution would be to meet outside school as usual to practise their dance steps. The peer mediators identified some risks and benefits. A major risk was that Tony might not want to be Kate's boyfriend since he seemed to enjoy the company of lots of girls. If Kate and Nicky did not explore this possibility, their quarrel might flare up again. The benefits were that they could go back to being best friends and continue to share their interest in dancing.

Step 3 The peer mediators invited Kate and Nicky to choose the solution with the highest probability of success. They agreed to meet and practise dancing steps. They also agreed that the future of Kate's relationship with Tony was separate from their friendship so that they were each free to chat with him or not.

Step 4 They agreed to try the plan of action and arranged to meet the next day after school. They also agreed that each was free to talk to Tony if the opportunity arose. The mediators wrote the plan of action down and checked that this was agreeable to both Kate and Nicky.

Step 5 They agreed to meet again with the mediators in a week's time to review progress and to evaluate how effective the action plan had been.

A week later, when they reconvened, the mediators were pleased to note that Kate and Nicky were very relaxed and friendly with each other. When they reviewed the week with them, Kate reported that she was no longer going out

continued overleaf

Case Study 8.2 continued

with Tony as she had seen him flirting with several other girls and realized that he was not serious about anyone. By contrast, she said that her friendship with Nicky was more important to her and that they were working hard preparing for their exams at the end of term. They had also found out that there was a lively new jazz club at school and had already made friends with some boys there. All agreed that the mediation had been helpful and that they did not need to meet again as they had reached a good solution.

Conferencing

This takes place when the dispute is more serious. The dispute may be between pupils (as above) or between pupil and teacher or between parent and teacher. Here the process is similar to mediation. The facilitator calls a conference, hears an account of what happened from each party, tries to enable agreement about what went wrong and what harm has been done, and moves towards a way of repairing the damage. The parties (as above) agree to make amends in some way acceptable to each one and agree to move on.

The conflict between Kate and Nicky was dealt with appropriately by the peer mediators and was well within their area of expertise. However, some peer relationship difficulties are too complex for peer mediators to resolve. This was the case in an ongoing dispute involving three primary school girls, Ruby, Shamina and Sophie. The bullying and spiteful behaviour that was escalating as a result of their quarrel had spilled out into the community since their families were now taking sides. Shamina's mother was beginning to stir up other parents at the school gate complaining about the aggressive behaviour of Sophie. Ruby's mother had twice approached the class teacher, Miss Rogers, voicing her concern that Ruby was being bullied by Sophie. Meanwhile, Sophie's mother had gone to the Deputy Head, Mrs Tahkvar, to report that Sophie was being bullied by Shamina. Each version of events seemed to contradict the other yet the problem was simmering away all the time and when a complaint came in that Sophie was engaged in racist taunting, Mrs Tahkkvar made the decision to adopt a restorative approach by involving the School Liaison Police Officer, Police Constable (PC) Sarah Reaney. We describe how the conference went in Case Study 8.3.

Case Study 8.3 Using a conference to resolve a friendship difficulty

PC Reaney made contact with the three girls and asked each one individually if they were willing to try a conference to see if their dispute could be resolved. She explained the process and reassured them that her intention was that each person who took part would feel positive about the experience by the end. Her hope was that the hurt and unhappiness caused by the arguments would be repaired and a new way forward found for all three. Each girl agreed to attend. PC Reaney then invited the parents of each girl to attend and, in a similar way, explained what the conference process would be like. She invited Miss Rogers too. They all arranged to meet the following Wednesday morning in a comfortable quiet room in the library. PC Reaney had thought through the seating plan in advance and arranged the chairs in a circle so that each girl sat with the member of her family who had agreed to attend. Miss Rogers sat opposite PC Reaney and in the middle of the family groups. There was a strained silence and the group atmosphere was tense.

Step 1 Setting the scene. Once they were all gathered together, PC Reaney ensured that everyone was comfortable and explained the process briefly again.

Step 2 Hearing the stories. She then asked each girl in turn to explain what had been happening and how she thought and felt at the time. First she invited Ruby to speak. Ruby said that when she first came to the school she had been really worried because everyone seemed to have a best friend except her. Then, to her great joy, Shamina had started to ask her to be her partner at games and they had discovered their shared interest in doing acrobatics. They had been to each other's homes to practise and everything had gone well until Sophie began to say really nasty things about her. The worst was when Sophie got a group of girls to chant repeatedly at break time, 'You're mean, mean, mean because you're white, white, white'. This made her feel so unhappy that after that she did not want to go to school anymore. Next, PC Reaney invited Shamina to give her version of events. Shamina said that before Ruby came, she had been best friends with Sophie and they had gone everywhere together but that every so often Sophie would suddenly cut her out and get all the other girls to ignore her. The final straw had been in October when Sophie invited everyone except Shamina to her birthday party. Shamina had been so hurt and angry about this as she could not understand how anyone could be so mean to her 'best friend'. Soon after that, Ruby joined the class and so Shamina had made sure that she befriended her, first to get even with Sophie but later because she really got on with Ruby, especially as Ruby was brilliant at acrobatics. Sophie was then invited to give her version of events. She said that she had always felt very jealous of Shamina as she was so pretty and petite. She also envied her skill at acrobatics and hated it that she, Sophie, was large and clumsy. She longed to look like Shamina but knew that this would never happen. She felt that it was unfair that everything good always happened to Shamina so she enjoyed making her unhappy over the birthday party. She felt that paid her back for being such a show-off. It served her right. Then when Ruby joined the class, she felt very

continued overleaf

Case Study 8.3 continued

jealous that here was another very pretty, slender girl who could do Arab springs, the splits and cartwheels with ease – all the things that she could never do. She could see that Ruby did not have very many friends as she was new, so it was easy to put her down. Sophie went bright red as she admitted this and sobbed, 'I never meant to hurt her. It's just that nobody knows how awful it is to be big and clumsy!' Sophie added, 'I wish that Shamina could be my friend again. It was all right before she came to the school' (glaring angrily at Ruby).

Step 3 Moving forward. PC Reaney congratulated all three for being so open and honest and went on, 'OK we have heard what each of you had to say and how we felt. We have heard about a lot of hurt feelings and anger. It is time for us now to try to find a way forward. Do you have any ideas on how things might be put right?' After a long silence, Ruby said, 'Perhaps we could all stop doing mean things to each other and hurting each other'. Shamina added, 'Perhaps we could start to think nice things about each other'. Sophie said, 'Perhaps we could all be friends'. Shamina looked down at the floor and made no reply.

Step 4 Coming to an agreement. PC Reaney asked the group, 'What do you think about these ideas? Let's take them in turn. What about not doing mean things any more?' They all agreed that this would certainly make life easier. 'What else would you need to do?' Shamina pointed out that Sophie had lots of friends and smiled at her for the first time. Sophie looked pleased at this comment and replied that she was glad that Shamina had noticed. PC Reaney then asked Sophie directly, 'I wonder how far you can make a person be friends with you? How would that make you feel?' After a silence, Sophie agreed that you could not force anyone like that and that she would feel bad. PC Reaney said, 'But you have a lot of influence with the other girls. There is quite a choice of girls for you to be friends with. Is that not the case?' Again Sophie looked pleased and said, 'Well actually I have been playing quite a lot with Amina and we really like each other'. PC Reaney went on, 'So what else might we do to make things better?' After some more discussion, Sophie agreed that she would leave Ruby and Shamina alone for the time being and play with some of the other girls instead. Ruby and Shamina agreed to respect this decision. PC Reaney asked the girls if they would like her to write this down as a sort of contract. They all said that they would.

Step 5 Closure. PC Reaney congratulated the three girls for all their hard work. She checked out how each was feeling and invited them to say anything to the other members of the group. Ruby said directly to Sophie, 'You did make me very unhappy but now I understand a bit why you did it'. Sophie smiled back and said, 'I am really sorry for what I did but now I feel that I know you a lot better than before. It is helpful to have our contract and I will really try to stick with it'. Shamina said, 'I can see now how easy it is to hurt people even when you don't mean to do it'. The whole mood of the group had changed and everyone, including the parents and Miss Rogers, looked relaxed and relieved.

Case Study 8.3 was about peer group relationships. Note that PC Reaney did not blame anyone but that, nevertheless, the girls did show awareness of the impact, often painful, of their actions on others. Sophie in particular showed some remorse and shame at her spiteful actions. However, PC Reaney did not dwell on these feelings. Instead she found ways to build up Sophie's self-esteem and to reintegrate her into the peer group. Both Ruby and Shamina showed their capacity to forgive and move on. But this came naturally from them. It was not forced by PC Reaney.

Conferencing can also be used very effectively to avoid exclusions (as in Case Study 8.1) or as part of reintegration following exclusion. In the next case study (Case Study 8.4) we see an example of how a trained facilitator was able to resolve a dispute between a pupil and his teacher through the process of bringing the relevant parties together to agree a solution in which the wrongdoer (in this case Paul) acknowledged the impact of his actions on other people and apologized to the teacher (Mrs Bryan) without losing face. All parties agreed a strategy to put the difficulty behind them and so were able to move on and relate to one another in a new and much more productive way. The conferencing process prevented Paul from being excluded from school and, in fact, reintegrated him into the school community.

Case Study 8.4 Ongoing aggression between Paul and his teachers

Paul Warner, who joined Year 9 after being excluded from his previous school for aggressive behaviour, quickly became known for his disruptive behaviour in class. Finally he was excluded again for swearing abusively at his English teacher, Mrs Bryan. The school arranged for Mr White, a local youth worker, trained in conferencing, to convene a conference as a key part of the process of trying to reintegrate Paul back into school. His mother, Mrs Warner, attended the conference as well as Mrs Bryan. During the conference Paul stated that all the teachers seemed to hate him and that they had all heard bad things about him from the teachers at his last school so he had no chance right from the start. He said that Mrs Bryan in particular despised him and laughed at his accent in front of his mates. He also admitted that he had been trying to impress the others as he was finding it difficult to make new friends in the school. Mrs Bryan said that in fact she did like him and provided some examples of times when she had praised his writing and his performance in a class role play. She said that she knew how difficult it could be coming into a class in the middle of term. Mrs Warner asked Paul how he would have felt if someone had sworn at him in the way that he did to Mrs Bryan. He said that he would be very upset and angry. Mrs Warner then said that she felt ashamed that her son could use such language and behave so badly to his teacher. She added that she believed that he could do a lot better and that moving to a new school was like a fresh start for him. Paul looked very embarrassed. He said that he had not known that his mother believed in him and had only remembered her shouting at him when

continued overleaf ⌐

Case Study 8.4 continued

he was excluded before. Prompted by Mr White, he agreed that it was not
necessary to swear at Mrs Bryan and then apologized to her. She accepted his
apology. She also said that she had set aside some examples of his creative
work to show Mrs Warner at the parents' evening the following week. Mr
White then asked him if there were any ways in which he could have behaved
differently in the English class. He agreed to talk to Mrs Bryan one to one if in
the future he felt that she was not treating him fairly. The conference ended on
a positive note with all parties agreeing that they had been heard and that they
felt able to communicate with one another more positively as a result. Paul kept
to his word and was able to voice feelings of insecurity to Mrs Bryan. Paul
began to enjoy English lessons and Mrs Bryan took care to praise him for his
involvement in drama and creative writing. Mrs Warner was delighted to see his
work at the parents' evening. Other staff noticed a marked improvement in his
attitude towards the school.

Benefits of Restorative Practice

The School

There is a growing body of evidence that shows how effective restorative
approaches are in reducing school violence. For example, trials of conferencing in Australian schools (Cameron and Thorsborne, 2001) found that
the majority of participants were generally very positive about the experience of taking part in a conference; victims felt safer after the conference
and perpetrators felt cared for during the conference and able to make a
fresh start. Over 80 per cent of perpetrators did not re-offend during the
trial period.

The national evaluation of the Restorative Justice in Schools Programme
in the UK (Youth Justice Board, 2004) provides strong evidence that the
method works when it is systematically implemented and embedded in
school practices and policies. This nationwide programme was developed to
tackle exclusions, truancy, bullying, violence and other forms of antisocial
behaviour. Pupil surveys found that there were important improvements in
the attitudes of pupils in those schools that had implemented restorative
justice using a whole-school approach. Staff surveys found that teachers
believed that restorative approaches improved the school, especially in
those schools that had adopted a whole-school approach. Ninety-two per
cent of conferences resulted in lasting agreements being made between the
parties and there was a high degree of satisfaction among the pupils who
had participated. Ninety-three per cent of pupils believed that the process
was fair and that justice had been done. There was a significant improve-

ment in pupil behaviour in those schools that implemented restorative practice and this was most marked in those where the approach was well integrated into the school's behaviour management policy, staff in-service training (INSET) and other forms of training.

Participants

Victims and perpetrators usually report that they benefit mutually from restorative practices. They each feel more confident in themselves and appreciate it that the school cared about the wrong that was done. They also report greater insights into why young people bully others and why some people are bullied. The most frequently mentioned benefits are:

- an increase in empowerment;
- a greater sense that someone hears issues and attends to them;
- an opportunity to make amends and then move on.

Box 8.1 Pupil views on the process from the Youth Justice Board (YJB) evaluation (YJB, 2004)

We all told the truth. I think it was because we were all in the room together and listening to what everybody was saying … I'm glad I didn't tell fibs because it was all sorted out in the end. (Year 7 girl)

We both had the chance to tell our side of things without being interrupted. It made a change for adults to listen to us. I felt respected, as a person, rather than being treated as a child and told what to do. (Year 8 boy)

There are also useful links with other systems, such as external training agencies (for example, the Youth Justice Board), and non-governmental organizations (NGOs) (for example, Conflict Practitioners UK), each of which offers potential for wider dissemination of the concept of restorative practice, through presentations at conferences, publication of achievements in newsletters and opportunities to meet and learn from others.

School Staff

School staff frequently report that the school environment becomes safer and more caring following the introduction of restorative practices, and that peer relationships in general improve. They report that the presence of restorative practices:

- empowers victims and reintegrates perpetrators;
- makes it more acceptable for pupils to report violence;
- reduces the occurrence of everyday conflicts;
- enables pupils to resolve conflicts in a peaceful way;

- makes the environment feel safer, with the playground being a happier place for pupils to be;
- enhances the reputation of the school in the local community.

Box 8.2 The impact on schools of a restorative practice programme (YJB, 2004)

In one school there was a 16 per cent reduction in pupils reporting that they had been hit or kicked by other pupils, and a 9 per cent reduction in theft.

In another, there was a 14 per cent reduction in racist name-calling and a 9 per cent reduction in pupils being isolated by others.

In another there was an 18 per cent decrease in pupils' perception that bullying was a serious problem in their school and an 11 per cent reduction in pupils thinking that telling a teacher about bullying was 'grassing'.

The degree to which the school integrates restorative practice into the whole-school policy as strategy is key to its success. The active support of the head teacher or a senior leadership figure is a crucial factor.

Activities for the Training Event

For this event we recommend that the facilitator should be trained and experienced in mediation and conferencing. The facilitator can then enable participants to practise the skills of mediation in Activities 8.1 and 8.2 and, finally, demonstrate a conference in Activity 8.3.

Activity 8.1 Freeze Frame (50 minutes)

Purpose
- To learn that conflicts can start with something quite simple.
- To explore the emotional impact when a conflict escalates.

Materials
  None.

Procedure
Ask participants to work in pairs to discuss a real conflict that they have had with another person. There are two roles. A tells the narrative of their experience of conflict; B listens to A's story. At the end of the story, B asks A to 'freeze frame' the worst moment as if a digital versatile disc (DVD) had been paused at that particular point in time. B invites A to hold that moment and to experience the physical sensations and emotions of that moment. B then asks A to move out of the freeze frame and to describe what was experienced. A and B then change roles and repeat the activity. Give the pairs 10 minutes each.

Discussion

The pairs are asked to return to the large group. Participants are invited to demonstrate their 'freeze frames' if they are willing. In the plenary, the facilitator asks the pairs to share some of the experiences that they had while doing this activity. The group collectively discusses the varying nature of the emotional impact of conflict on different people. This exercise can be very useful in developing awareness of the physical sensations that accompany heightened emotions. Allow 20 minutes for this debriefing in plenary.

Activity 8.2 Mediation (50 minutes)

Purpose
- To give participants the opportunity to practise the skills of mediation between two people in dispute.

Materials
Activity Handout 8.1 Five Steps to Mediation, p. 108.
Activity Handout 8.2 Observer's Checklist, p. 109

Procedure

Participants work in groups of four or five. The groups each select one of the conflicts elicited in Activity 8.1. Each group decides on the roles that they are to take for the first round: two disputants; one mediator; one or two observers. The trainer goes through the five stages of mediation (Activity Handout 8.1 Five Steps to Mediation) and invites the groups to practise these steps in relation to the conflicts that they have selected. The observers make notes using Activity Handout 8.2 Observer's Checklist.

Discussion

Discussion takes place within the groups. Feedback is given by each person in order: disputants; observer(s); mediator. The groups explore what happened; how it felt; were there any difficult emotions? How did the different roles experience the solution? Were there any other ways that the mediators could have handled the dispute?

Activity 8.3 Running a Conference (50 minutes)

Materials
Activity Handout 8.3 The Dispute
Activity Handout 8.4 Debriefing a Conference

Procedure

The trainer takes on the role of conference facilitator. We suggest that the conference focuses on one of the disputes in Activity Handout 8.3 but the trainer may prefer to select a real-life conflict from their own experience, taking care to protect the identity of all those involved. Members of the group are invited to take a range of roles to include the victim, friends/relatives of the victim, the perpetrator, friends/relatives of the perpetrator, and observers. The trainer demonstrates how such a conference might be run.

Discussion

Finally, the whole group reconvenes in plenary to discuss their experiences of observing or actively taking part in a conference using Activity Handout 8.4, Debriefing a Conference.

Further Reading

Cameron, L. and Thorsborne, M. (2001) 'Restorative justice and school discipline: mutually exclusive?', in H. Strang and J. Braithwaite (eds), *Restorative Justice and Civil Society*. Cambridge: Cambridge University Press. pp. 180–94.

Morrison, B. (2003) 'Regulating safe school communities: being responsive and restorative', *Journal of Educational Administration*, 41(6): 689–704.

Wachtel, T. and McCold, T. (2001) 'Restorative justice in everyday life: beyond the formal ritual', in H. Strang and J. Braithwaite (eds), *Restorative Justice and Civil Society*. Cambridge: Cambridge University Press, pp 114–29.

Websites

Better Behaviours Scotland, www.betterbehaviourscotland.gov.uk
Conflict Practitioners, www.conflictpractitioners.org
International Institute of Restorative Practices, www.iirp.org and www.real justice.org
Peer Support Networker, www.ukobservatory.com
Restorative Justice Consortium, www.restorativejustice.org.uk
Restorative Justice Online, www.restorativejustice.org/
TeacherNet, www.teachernet.gov.uk
Thames Valley Police, www.thamesvalley.police.uk
Transforming Conflict, www.transformingconflict.org
UK Observatory for the Promotion of Non-violence, www.ukobservatory.com
Youth Justice Board for England and Wales, www.youth-justice-board.gov.uk

Resources

Cole, T. (2000) *Kids Helping Kids*. Victoria, BC: Peer Resources.

Cowie, H. and Wallace, P. (2000) *Peer Support in Action*. London: Sage Publications.

Hopkins, B. (2004) *Just Schools*. London: Jessica Kingsley.

Petch, B. and Withers, T. (2006) *Peer Mediation: Guidance Notes for Schools*. Solihull Metropolitan Borough Council, PO Box 20, Council House, Solihull, West Midlands B91 3QU, UK.

Salter, K. and Twidle, R. (2005) *The Learning Mentor's Source and Resource Book*. London: Paul Chapman Publishing.

Zehr, H. (2002) *The Little Book of Restorative Justice*. Intercourse, PA: Good Books.

Evaluations

Youth Justice Board (2004) *National Evaluation of the Restorative Justice in Schools Programme*. London: YJB, www.youth-justice-board.gov.uk

Activity Handout 8.1 Five Steps to Mediation

Stage 1 Identify the problem

Make the disputants feel comfortable. Explain what the process of conferencing entails. Invite each participant to describe their view of the problem situation without interruption, stating feelings as well as facts.

The facilitator clarifies the needs and interests of each party, using statements like, 'My understanding of what you said is this … '.

Each party is asked to summarize what the other said.

The facilitator summarizes what each has said.

Stage 2 Explore options

Each party states what ideally they would like to happen and is invited to suggest possible solutions. The facilitator notes possible risks and benefits.

Stage 3 Take account of risks and benefits

The facilitator invites each party to think about the outcomes of the suggested solutions. Each is invited to explore possible risks and possible benefits of the proposed solutions.

Stage 4 Make a plan of action

Each party considers which solutions are likely to meet the needs of both. They are asked to select one or two possible solutions. The facilitator clarifies what each party agrees to do and by when. The facilitator then draws up a written agreement of future actions which is signed by all present. Both parties shake hands.

Stage 5 Review and evaluate

The parties agree to meet to review outcomes and to evaluate what happened. They agree to renegotiate as appropriate. The facilitator praises each party for successes and summarizes in context the values of cooperation and trust. Close the meeting by acknowledging that progress has been made (even if complete resolution has not been reached). Invite each person to reflect on how they might each behave differently in the future.

Activity Handout 8.2 Observer's Checklist

* **What messages were conveyed by the mediator's eyes, gestures, body position, facial expression?**

  _____

  _____

  _____

  _____

  _____

  _____

* **How appropriate was the voice of the mediator?**

  _____

  _____

  _____

  _____

  _____

* **How interested did the mediator appear in the supportee's problem?**

  _____

  _____

  _____

  _____

  _____

  _____

Provide evidence for each of your comments

Activity Handout 8.3 The Dispute

An argument has flared up between two families in the school community after one family held a very noisy party that ran late into the night and refused to turn the music down despite repeated, angry protests from the neighbours. This family conflict has spilled over into the school environment and has evolved into fighting between the four children, two from each family. It is further complicated since the two girls, Janice and Tracy, used to be best friends. Other pupils have become involved and the conflict is acted out during every break. The school decides to convene a conference to try to resolve the dispute and achieve a peaceful resolution. The four pupils and their family members are invited to attend.

David, until recently a model pupil, has started hanging around with a new group of friends. This group has been involved in fighting with a neighbourhood gang from a different school after members of that gang sent offensive messages by text to David's friend Matthew insulting Matthew's girlfriend. Matthew is inciting the others to take revenge. The arguments have escalated and take place at the bus station on the main road that lies between the two schools. Everyone knows that the gang members carry knives. David is having doubts about whether it is a good idea to take revenge but his new friends think he is a coward. He talks to his parents who contact the school. The head teacher has also had complaints from passengers at the bus station so already knows about the situation. She decides to convene a conference facilitated by the school police liaison office.

Activity Handout 8.4 Debriefing a Conference

❖ **Did the activity address harms, needs and causes?**

❖ **Was it victim-oriented?**

❖ **Were perpetrators encouraged to take responsibility for what they did?**

❖ **Were all relevant stakeholders involved?**

❖ **Was there an opportunity for dialogue and participation in the decision-making process?**

❖ **Was the model respectful to all parties?**

The Support Group Method

Objectives

- To understand the role of the support group in addressing school violence.
- To be familiar with the skills involved in facilitating the Support Group Method.

What Is the Support Group Method?

This chapter introduces you to the Support Group Method (Maines and Robinson, 1997) – what it looks like, its benefits, and how you can train pupils and staff to implement it. The Support Group Method adopts a 'no-blame' approach. It aims to change the behaviour of children involved in bullying others by increasing their empathy for the bullied pupil's feelings and by making constructive use of group processes to offer care and support. The method adopts a problem-solving approach, gives responsibility to the group to solve the problem and to report back on progress at a subsequent review meeting. The method is controversial since, instead of punishing the perpetrators, it focuses on the emotions of the bullied pupil and on what the support group can do (including the bully) to make that person feel better. By focusing on feeling, attention is drawn away from who did what to whom and who was to blame.

Why Does it Work?

The major task of the support group is to alleviate the suffering of the victim through the powerful tool of empathy and cooperative sharing in problem-solving. The facilitator achieves this by creating a non-judgemental forum – the support group – in which bullies, bystanders and defenders can collectively reflect on the impact of their behaviour on others, and explore ways of changing it (Table 9.1). Perpetrators and bystanders alike can express their own thoughts and feelings openly. Most importantly, the process changes the power structure within the group by taking away support for negative behaviours and by empowering people to do something to help a peer in distress. This is likely to make them feel positive about themselves and kinder towards others.

Table 9.1 The Support Group Method: five steps for implementation

1 Meet with the bullied pupil
(a) Explain the process
(b) Focus on his or her feelings
(c) Ask for permission to use the method
(d) Ask for the names of six to eight pupils who might be included
(e) Invite the bullied pupil to write a piece or draw a picture that captures their feelings
2 Select the group
(a) Consult with the class teacher
(b) Include representatives of the entire group as agreed with the bullied pupil
3 Convene the meeting
(a) Explain the problem to the group
(b) Avoid detail and blame
(c) Facilitate empathy for the bullied pupil's feelings
(d) Invite the group to make suggestions
(e) Allow the group to take responsibility for the action plan
4 Review one week later
(a) Check how the bullied pupil is feeling and whether he or she has experienced change
(b) Check on the support group's progress and the outcomes
5 Follow-up
(a) Convene another group meeting if necessary
(b) Review again as in Step 4
(c) Check outcomes with class teacher and parents

Case Study 9.1 Stephen: an isolated boy

Stephen, a Year 7 pupil with special learning needs, was becoming increasingly isolated. He was smaller than the others and did not seem to have any friends at all. He found it hard to work in groups and was almost always alone during break times. He was very subdued during the meeting with Mrs Miles, the school nurse, trained as a Support Group Method facilitator. He told her that James and Clark were always taunting him about his size and calling him insulting names. They said in particular that his ears were too big, often shouted 'Rabbit!' as he went past or silently mimed large rabbit ears in class. Recently, they had been tripping him up in the corridors and deliberately crashing into him as he walked about the school. As a result, he had become reluctant to go to school and was frequently absent with minor physical complaints. His school work was deteriorating. At the initial interview with Mrs Miles, Stephen spoke in a very quiet voice. His eyes were downcast and he looked extremely miserable. Mrs Miles listened carefully to his account and then asked him to help her select a group of pupils who could support him.

continued opposite

Case Study 9.1 continued

With clear misgivings, he agreed to invite James and Clark and, with greater optimism, also David and Jason who were boys that he would have liked to be friends with. Mrs Miles suggested Oz who, according to Stephen, had sometimes intervened when James and Clark were being especially nasty, and he agreed that Oz could be a very useful member of the group. She also recommended Gemma and Sarah who had been trained as peer tutors and who could help Stephen to catch up with his reading. He was happy with this choice too.

---

1 *Meeting with the bullied pupil*. The adult who will facilitate the support group (in this case the school nurse, Mrs Miles) arranges to meet with the bullied pupil (in this case, Stephen) – either alone or, if the young person prefers, with a friend or parent. Mrs Miles asks if it is all right to make notes during the meeting and also checks whether there are any details that Stephen does not want to share with the others. Helped by sensitive questioning on the part of Mrs Miles, Stephen describes what happened, who took part in the bullying episode and who was helpful, or might be helpful in the future. It is important at this point to focus on Stephen's feelings. Sometimes this account can best be described in writing or through drawings.

2 *Select the group*. When Stephen has told his story, Mrs Miles proposes the idea of a support group and consults with him about which people should be selected to form the support group and about when it is best to meet. Mrs Miles also explains that Stephen will not attend the group meeting. As agreed with Stephen, Mrs Miles forms a group consisting of six to eight pupils that he nominated in the meeting (Step 1), including those involved in the bullying episode (bully, assistants of the bully, and defenders of the victim) and bystanders who seem to have the potential to be supportive and friendly. Mrs Miles checks with the form tutor about the proposed composition of the group.

3 *Convene the group*. Mrs Miles begins by saying, 'We are here to help Stephen who is feeling unhappy … You have all been chosen because you are all able to help'. The atmosphere should be non-judgemental so that each one can address the issue as a problem-solving task. Once they understand the rationale for being in the group, most pupils are able to be open about what happened and how they might change things for the better. Mrs Miles gives an account of what has happened and, by focusing on how Stephen might be feeling, begins the process of eliciting empathy. Common responses include: 'But Stephen is so irritating …' or 'We did not know how hurt he would be' or 'It was partly his fault'. Mrs Miles emphasizes that the purpose of the group meeting is to solve

the problem, not to apportion blame. The group has the opportunity to take joint responsibility for the situation. In a wider sense, the group is encouraged to understand that no one needs to feel unhappy at school. The group is reminded that its collective responsibility is to make Stephen happier. Mrs Miles asks members of the group if they have any ideas about how to help Stephen and notes them down. Common solutions include: 'Ask Stephen to sit with us', 'Walk to school with Stephen', 'Ignore it when Stephen is annoying', 'Ask Stephen to join in our games', 'Stop calling him names' or 'Choose Stephen as a partner for games'. If the group is reluctant to offer solutions, Mrs Miles can prompt some suggestions. The group must own the plan of action. Mrs Miles thanks everyone for their problem-solving skill once the group has agreed on a plan of action. She arranges a review meeting with the group a week later to share progress. It is essential that the meeting ends with a sense of group ownership of the plan of action.

Box 9.1 The support group meeting

Between six and eight pupils make an ideal size of group which is small enough for good interaction and large enough to be representative of those involved in the bullying situation. The group must include the main perpetrators (in this case James), one or two supporters of the bully (in this case Clark), some bystanders (in this case Gemma and Sarah, David and Jason) and, if possible, someone who has already defended the victim (in this case Oz). The supportive processes of the group experience give each member the opportunity to feel empathy for Stephen and to act in a more pro-social way collectively. This can be a very rewarding experience for everyone.

---

4 *Review meetings.* Mrs Miles arranges to meet Stephen a week later to review progress, with the focus being on positive things that have happened. Mrs Miles praises Stephen for his efforts. This meeting usually lasts for no longer than five minutes. Mrs Miles then meets the support group and invites members to review the group's contribution to the resolution of the problem. Mrs Miles then thanks the group for its efforts to make Stephen happier. They are asked if they would like to hold one more review meeting; often children and young people are very keen for this to happen.

5 *Follow-up.* If necessary, a follow-up meeting of the support group takes place. The format is the same as Step 3. Mrs Miles also finds an opportunity to feed back to Stephen's parents. Young (1998) emphasizes the need to involve parents of the victim at this stage and to ask for their views on any changes that they have noticed in their child. This is often very helpful in rebuilding their relationship with the school. In this case, Mrs

Miles reported back to the school's pastoral care team mee
to establish the Support Group Method firmly as a ke
whole-school community approach to counteracting vic
reported back to the local CAMHS team meeting ﹍
professionals linked to the school were aware of its effectiveᴵ﹍
could recommend it following diagnosis of a young person's mentaɪ
health needs.

Benefits of the Support Group Method

Research Findings

Many pupils and teachers report that they like the method.

Group members usually report that they benefit from the group process, that they feel more confident in themselves and that they learn to value other people more. The most frequently mentioned benefits are:

- it is fair;
- they are empowered to help;
- they are proud that they helped to stop the bullying.

Bullied pupils report that:

- they feel safer as a result of the help they receive;
- they feel understood;
- they feel that people care about their feelings.

Bullies report that:

- they had not realized how much hurt they caused;
- they are glad that they were not told off;
- they are now sorry for what they did;
- they are glad to be able to take positive action.

Case Study 9.2 Angela: a girl who reinforced bullying behaviour

Angela, aged 9, and her best friend, June, had been picking on Sudha for weeks. It was great fun to pass secret notes about her round the class. It was even better to poke fun at her clothes and imitate her accent. They used to have a laugh about it afterwards within their own group. Most recently, June had a brilliant idea, 'Let's send Sudha horrible text messages and watch her face when she reads them!' When Miss Bevan asked Angela and June to take part in a special meeting about Sudha, they were sure that they were going to be told off.

continued overleaf

Case Study 9.2 continued

Angela saw how June prepared herself by folding her arms and putting on her tough face – the one that made you really scared – and saying under her breath, 'I'll get you for this, Sudha, you sneaky, lying bitch!' Angela tried to sit in the same way as June, though she did not feel tough inside. Actually, she was really angry at Sudha for telling and could not wait for June to get the others to join them in taking revenge. To her surprise, Miss Bevan smiled in a welcoming way to everyone and explained that they were all going to work together to help Sudha feel happier at school. She then asked them to imagine how they might feel if everyone kept on picking on them and laughing at them. Angela was sure that they would all just say nothing but she was surprised when quite a few of them said how bad they would feel. That made Angela feel quite uncomfortable. She did not dare look up. Then Miss Bevan showed them a DVD which showed different children offering to do helpful things to support someone who was feeling sad. Miss Bevan then asked the group if they had any ideas for helping Sudha. There was a bit of a silence. Angela thought to herself, 'Well no one would want to help Sudha'. But again to her surprise most of the others started to come up with suggestions. For example, Katie and Ellie said, 'We could sit with her at lunch!' Nasra said, 'I'll walk with her to school. She only lives round the corner'. Angela looked over at June and saw that she was bright red and looked very embarrassed. June did not say much but in the end, with Miss Bevan's encouragement, agreed to leave Sudha alone until the next meeting a week later. So Angela agreed to do the same as June. Angela was amazed at how relieved she felt when Miss Bevan smiled and said, 'What a great idea. Let's see how it goes!' That was all!

When the group met the following week, everyone reported back on what they had done and they all looked so pleased at their success. All Angela and June had done was to leave Sudha alone but Miss Bevan seemed as pleased with that as anything. Deep down Angela felt quite ashamed about sending those texts. She had no idea that Sudha would take it so badly. Somehow now it did not seem quite such a funny thing to do.

Teachers frequently report that the school environment becomes safer and more caring following the introduction of the Support Group Method, and that peer relationships in general improve. They report that the presence of the Support Group Method:

- has an impact on the whole school community;
- encourages positive relationships among pupils;
- gives pupils useful strategies for behaving differently to one another;
- restores relationships rather than leaves them in tatters;
- works even with entrenched negative behaviours;
- directly challenges the bullies, unlike many interventions.

Research findings are positive. For example, Young (1998) and Young and

Holdorf (2003), who have used the method extensively with pupils who have emotional and behavioural difficulties, found that in 80 per cent of primary school cases treated through the Support Group Method there was an immediate success; in 14 per cent of cases delayed or partial success, and in only 6 per cent of cases the victim reported that the bullying continued, or that he or she was bullied by different pupils. These researchers observed a similar outcome in secondary school referrals. Young explains the success of the method in terms of the dynamics of the group and the individuals within it. She argues that the Support Group Method creates the optimum conditions for the bystander who might otherwise do nothing to act helpfully towards a peer in distress. She notes that individuals are more likely to help when:

- they have been asked to help and have agreed;
- they know that the need for action is clear;
- they have been given some responsibility for their actions;
- they have been reassured and convinced that their action is appropriate;
- they have witnessed the harm done to the victim and have had their empathy for that person aroused;
- they know that they will receive some feedback on their actions;
- they feel uncomfortable about the pain and hurt caused by the perpetrators and by their own inaction in the past.

Young proposes that the support group has a purpose that goes beyond any individual member. The Support Group Method alters the balance so that the benefits for helping the victim outweigh the costs. Young (1998) notes the importance of convincing parents that the Support Group Method has a high success rate. Parents of a bullied child are understandably upset and angry. Often they wish for a punitive reaction on the part of the school towards the perpetrators. In Young's experience, however, parents are generally ready to give the method a try, since their main wish is that their child's suffering ends.

Sullivan et al. (2004) actively promoted the Support Group Method in their Australian pack of anti-bullying materials. Sullivan (2000) clarifies the method's philosophy as one that appeals to the bully's better nature, on the one hand, and alters the social dynamics of the bullying system, on the other. As he points out, bullies tend to see their victims as worthless people or even as 'non-people'. The great achievement of the Support Group Method is to 'rehumanize' the situation by focusing on the feelings of all those who are involved.

This means that the first key outcome of the method is to create a context which evokes sympathy for the victim's feelings on the part of the bully, encourages the bully to imagine what it must have felt like to be a victim, encourages the bully to express remorse and, in the best scenarios, enables that bully to realize that the behaviour is wrong. The positive thing is that this realization happens not through punishment and blame but because the bully now perceives the bullied pupil as a person with feelings.

The second key outcome is that the collective process of tapping into feelings extends to the wider peer group. It is not simply left to the bully/bullies to change but includes the onlookers, the bystanders and the potential defenders. Within the safety of the support group, the pupils can explore their own feelings about bullying without disapproval from the facilitator and discover the empowering effects of reaching out to someone else and offering help. This shifts the power base away from the bullies. The issue then becomes one of shared concern.

Sullivan also notes that, where schools have extended the number of times that the support group meets in order to discuss bullying issues in general, the (former) bullies become the staunchest defenders of the school's anti-bullying policy.

Smith, Howard and Thompson (2007), sound a note of caution. While they report widespread satisfaction with the method, they also note substantial variation in the way that the support groups are implemented. Our view, however, is that these findings simply confirm the flexibility of this powerful method.

Activities for the Training Event

Activity 9.1 Meeting the Bullied Pupil (60 minutes)

Purpose
• To practise the skills of facilitating the initial meeting.

Materials
   Case Study 9.1 Stephen: an isolated child.

Procedure
The facilitator asks for a volunteer to role play Stephen, a bullied pupil. The volunteer is given Case Study 9.1 to read. The facilitator then demonstrates how the initial meeting might be run. After that, participants divide into threes in which one person plays Stephen, one the facilitator and the third the observer. In the groups, they practise the running of the initial meeting with the bullied pupil. After the practice meeting, each participant reflects back to the trio how they experienced it.

Discussion
Take feedback from the whole group by asking them to share their experiences of role playing the initial meeting. The facilitator draws attention to the fact that the group already has the skills and qualities to empathise with the victims and to offer a solution.

Activity 9.2 Convening the Support Group (60 minutes)

Purpose
• To practise the skills of facilitating the support group meeting.

Materials
Case Study 9.1 Stephen: an isolated child.

Procedure
The facilitator asks for volunteers to role play the bullies, the bystanders and potential defenders. The facilitator then demonstrates how the support group meeting might be run. After that, volunteers take it in turn to facilitate a support group. After the practice support group, each participant reflects back to the group how they experienced it and the group in turn offers constructive criticism.

Discussion
Take feedback from the group by asking them to share their experiences of facilitating the support group meeting.

Activity 9.3 Discussing the Value of the Support Group (30 minutes)

Purpose
• To practise the skills of critique in the context of the support group meeting.

Materials
Feedback from Activities 9.1 and 9.2.

Procedure
Discuss in small groups the individual experiences of different roles within the support group. Explore the strengths of the method and where and with whom it might best be used.

Discussion
In the plenary, the facilitator summarizes issues arising from the small group discussions. The facilitator then invites the group to reflect on how they can encourage pupils in the support groups to act in helpful ways towards the target pupil.

Further Reading

Rigby, K. (1997) *Bullying in Schools and What to Do About It*. London: Jessica Kingsley.

Resources

Department for Education and Skills (2000) *Bullying: Don't Suffer in Silence. An Anti-bullying Pack for Schools.* 2nd edn. London: DfES.

Maines, B. and Robinson, G. (1997) *Crying for Help: The No Blame Approach to Bullying.* Bristol: Lucky Duck Publishing.

Sullivan, K., Cleary, M. and Sullivan, G. (2004) *Bullying in Secondary Schools.* London: Paul Chapman Publishing.

Evaluations

McGrath, H. and Stanley, M. (2006) 'A comparison of two non-punitive approaches to bullying', in H. McGrath and T. Noble (eds), *Bullying solutions: Evidence-based approaches to bullying in Australian schools.* Frenchs Forest, NSW: Pearson. pp.189–201.

Smith, P.K., Howard, S. and Thompson, F. (2007) 'Use of the Support Group Method to tackle bullying', *Pastoral Care in Education*, June, 4–13.

Sullivan, K. (2000) *The Anti-Bullying Handbook.* Oxford: Oxford University Press.

Young, S. (1998) 'The support group approach to bullying in schools', *Educational Psychology in Practice*, 14: 32–9.

Young, S. and Holdorf, G. (2003) 'Using solution focused brief therapy in individual referrals for bullying', *Educational Psychology in Practice*, 19: 271–82.

10 | Whole-school community checklist: promoting a safe school environment

We end the book with a whole-school evaluation checklist and a school climate checklist for pupils that we hope will enable you to identify the areas on which you need to work to monitor your progress in addressing the issue of violence in your school and in promoting a positive school environment. You can use these topics to structure evaluation meetings or as an individual exercise to kick-start your needs analysis. If you use these checklists, please inform us of your findings.

I Understanding the issue of school violence

	In place	Not in place	Working towards
We regularly discuss the nature and definition of school violence during lessons and assemblies and staff meetings	[ ]	[ ]	[ ]
We are aware of the various forms that school violence can take, including physical, psychological and social	[ ]	[ ]	[ ]
We are aware of the levels of influence on violent behaviour from individual, to inter-personal, to community and to the wider society	[ ]	[ ]	[ ]
We are aware of risk factors that influence violent behaviour and the extent to which we can minimize them	[ ]	[ ]	[ ]
We are aware of protective factors that influence violent behaviour and the extent to which we can strengthen them	[ ]	[ ]	[ ]
We gather information about school violence from local, national and international sources	[ ]	[ ]	[ ]
We are aware of the range of strategies that have been developed to prevent violence	[ ]	[ ]	[ ]

Sources of evidence:

Documentary evidence recording the content of assemblies across the school year and the promotion of non-violence across the curriculum

Training for pupils, staff and other adults from the whole-school community to address school violence

Named persons responsible for coordinating and regularly updating information on school violence

Records of links with outside agencies

2 Commitment to the promotion of non-violence through a whole-school policy

	In place	Not in place	Working towards
We have a policy in place that commits us to addressing the issue of school violence	[ ]	[ ]	[ ]
Our anti-violence policy was drawn up through a process of consultation with representatives from all sections of the whole-school community, including pupils	[ ]	[ ]	[ ]
Our policy makes reference to desired standards of behaviour	[ ]	[ ]	[ ]
We have developed a variety of methods to ensure that the anti-violence policy is easily and actively read and understood by all members of the school community	[ ]	[ ]	[ ]
Our anti-violence policy is regularly monitored and evaluated	[ ]	[ ]	[ ]
We have a system in place for documenting and investigating complaints about violence and safety issues	[ ]	[ ]	[ ]
Other policies such as our Behaviour Management Policy, Anti-bullying Policy, Communication Policy, Equal Opportunities Policy, Child Protection Policy, PSHE Policy and Citizenship Policy reflect our commitment to the promotion of non-violence	[ ]	[ ]	[ ]

Sources of evidence:

Documentary evidence of whole-school community involvement such as minutes of staff meetings, governors' meetings, parent/teacher association meetings, class meetings, School Council meetings

Evidence of dissemination through posters, leaflets, newsletters, staff meetings, school assemblies, parents' meetings, governors' meetings

Evidence of a named governor aware of and involved in policy development, maintenance and review

Observations that demonstrate pupils', staff's and other adults' knowledge of expected standards of behaviour

Evidence of effective recording and documentation of behaviour which reflects aspects of the school policy

3 Working with relationships

	In place	Not in place	Working towards
We have created opportunities to celebrate positive achievements and success of pupils, staff and other members of the school community	[ ]	[ ]	[ ]
We involve the whole-school community in such celebrations	[ ]	[ ]	[ ]
We encourage staff and pupils to be appreciative of one another	[ ]	[ ]	[ ]
The school environment is attractive and there is a welcoming atmosphere for visitors to the school	[ ]	[ ]	[ ]
We regularly discuss values and relationships during lessons and assemblies	[ ]	[ ]	[ ]
A significant number of pupils and staff have been trained in conflict resolution	[ ]	[ ]	[ ]
A peer support system is in place	[ ]	[ ]	[ ]
Emotional literacy is taught and reinforced across the curriculum and in the staff room	[ ]	[ ]	[ ]
Restorative practices are in place both within and in partnership with outside agencies	[ ]	[ ]	[ ]
Staff and pupils are able to articulate their concerns and feelings in a safe way	[ ]	[ ]	[ ]
A culture of mutual respect and cooperation is fostered between staff, between pupils and between staff and pupils	[ ]	[ ]	[ ]

Sources of evidence:

Opportunities for pupils and staff to demonstrate their work and achievements, for example, through 'showing' assemblies, class meetings and displays

Observations of the school environment such as signs and directions, school displays and notice boards, and school prospectus and website

Evidence of procedures in place to address litter, graffiti and other damage to school property

Evidence of an effective pastoral support programme in place

Evidence of clearly articulated procedures in place to monitor staff and pupil disciplinary and grievance concerns

Evidence of named staff in place whom pupils can contact about safety and relationship issues

Use of pupils' message boxes

Observations of postive interactions among all members of the whole-school community

4 Managing behaviour positively

	In place	Not in place	Working towards
Specific opportunities are in place for pupils to think about changing their own behaviours	[ ]	[ ]	[ ]
Policies, procedures and practices are implemented consistently and with transparent fairness throughout all parts of the school	[ ]	[ ]	[ ]
Incentive to change is generated by pupils and based on their recognition that their choices have consequences	[ ]	[ ]	[ ]
All members of the school staff are aware of their social and moral responsibilities as positive role models and are willing to change their practice when necessary	[ ]	[ ]	[ ]
Opportunities are provided for pupils to extend their range of options/skills they have for managing their behaviour	[ ]	[ ]	[ ]
The development of pupil self-esteem is actively promoted	[ ]	[ ]	[ ]
All people in school are accountable for their behaviour, and there are mechanisms to communicate about this	[ ]	[ ]	[ ]
Parents are informed about the approaches the school is using to promote non-violence and are offered training (where appropriate) to support the work at home	[ ]	[ ]	[ ]
Parents are recognized as active partners helping their children to develop a range of positive behavioural strategies	[ ]	[ ]	[ ]
Opportunities are in place for the professional development of all staff, which includes the principles and promotion of non-violence	[ ]	[ ]	[ ]

Sources of evidence:

Evidence of availability of training for all pupils to understand and address school violence

Records of lesson and tutorial plans

Evidence that the Staff Handbook is available for all staff, including temporary staff, and updated regularly

Evidence that a school reward system is in place and understood and applied consistently by all staff

Evidence of an induction programme in place for all new pupils, parents and staff

Evidence of pupil-led initiatives in place such as a peer support system, a buddying/befriending system, a School Council

Opportunities for professional development for all staff

Evidence of procedures in place to support bullied pupils as well as witnesses and bystanders of violent behaviour

Evidence of procedures in place to help change the behaviour of pupils who engage in violence

Opportunities available for honest feedback through, for example, circle time

Evidence of a range of opportunities for pupils to demonstrate their achievements

Evidence that information is sent home by letter and newsletter and disseminated through meetings

Evidence that parents/carers are provided with information about the curriculum their children are being taught

Evidence of active parent/carer involvement through, for example, visits and sharing their knowledge and skills

5 Building sustainability

	In place	Not in place	Working towards
We have allocated resources (financial, human, organizational) to help us implement our policy	[ ]	[ ]	[ ]
We have made contact with outside partners in the community to help us maintain our anti-violence policy	[ ]	[ ]	[ ]
We keep regular contact with these partners through email and newsletters	[ ]	[ ]	[ ]
We initiate regular events such as conferences and workshops that involve all members of the whole-school community and outside partners	[ ]	[ ]	[ ]
We promote non-violence through the development of a school culture and ethos that is respectful and appreciative of one another and which celebrates diversity	[ ]	[ ]	[ ]
We have allocated school time for regular discussions on values and relationships at school, in the community and in society at large	[ ]	[ ]	[ ]
We evaluate new programmes to ensure that they are free from issues that might provoke violence	[ ]	[ ]	[ ]
We build a sense of ownership by involving representatives of all members of the school and its local community in our policies and practices	[ ]	[ ]	[ ]
We regularly conduct surveys and observations to check that staff and pupils feel safe in all parts of the school environment	[ ]	[ ]	[ ]
We actively seek out best practices and share them with the school and the community	[ ]	[ ]	[ ]
We have an action plan in place which ensures the regular monitoring and reviewing of existing policies, structures and practices for the promotion of non-violence	[ ]	[ ]	[ ]

Sources of evidence:

Documentary evidence of resource allocation such as an outline of staff responsibilities and a named member of staff coordinating policy development, implementation and review

Evidence of collaboration and partnership with outside agencies (see Chapter 3)

Documentary evidence recording the content of assemblies across the school year and the promotion of non-violence across the curriculum

Evidence of carrying out a needs analysis involving all members of the whole-school community (see Chapter 5)

Evidence of a school action plan

SCHOOL CLIMATE CHECKLIST (PRIMARY VERSION)
(adapted from Hutson and Myers, unpublished)

Please answer the following questions. There are no right or wrong answers; we want to know your thoughts. All of your answers will be treated confidentially, and will not be seen by anyone else at your school. Thank you for your help

SECTION 1: WHERE YOU LIVE

1: Do you like where you live?

Yes ☐   No ☐

2: Please indicate how much you agree or disagree with the following statements about your local area ...

	Agree	Disagree
The area is a friendly place to be	☐	☐
The area is a place where people look after each other	☐	☐
Most people in this area trust one other	☐	☐
There are lots of people in this area that I don't know	☐	☐
The area is unfriendly	☐	☐

SECTION 2: YOUR JOURNEY TO SCHOOL

3: How do you travel to school?

4: How safe do you feel travelling to and from school?

Very unsafe   A bit unsafe   Very safe

SECTION 3: YOUR SCHOOL

5: Is school a nice place to be?

Yes ☐   No ☐

6: Please indicate how much you agree or disagree with the following statements about your school ...

	Agree	Disagree
The school is a friendly place to be	☐	☐
The school is a place where people look after each other	☐	☐
Most people in this school trust one other	☐	☐
There are lots of people in this school that I don't know	☐	☐
The school is unfriendly	☐	☐

7: Have you ever played truant from school?

Yes ☐   No ☐

8: Have you ever been suspended or excluded from school?

Yes ☐   No ☐

9: How safe do you feel in the school toilets?

Very unsafe   A bit unsafe   Very safe

10: How safe do you feel in the corridors (for example, when going between lessons)?

Very unsafe   A bit unsafe   Very safe

11: How safe do you feel in lessons?

Very unsafe   A bit unsafe   Very safe

12: How safe do you feel in the school playground?

Very unsafe   A bit unsafe   Very safe

13: Where do you feel least safe and why?

_____

_____

14: Where do you feel most safe and why?

_____

_____

SECTION 4: NEGATIVE EXPERIENCES AT SCHOOL

12: Do you worry about being bullied at school?

A lot   A bit   Or not at all

13: Are you worried about being rejected or disliked by your friends?

A lot   A bit   Or not at all

14: In the last week, have you been threatened or intimidated in any way by anybody in this school?

A lot ☐   A bit ☐   Or not at all ☐

15: In the last week, has anyone stolen or damaged anything of yours at school?

Yes ☐   No ☐

16: When bad things happen, do you tell anyone?

Yes ☐   No ☐

17: If 'yes', who did you tell?

No one ☐
A friend or girlfriend or boyfriend ☐
A peer supporter ☐
A member of your family ☐
A teacher or other adult at school ☐
Other ☐

18: In the last week, have YOU upset other students by calling them hurtful names?

A lot ☐   A bit ☐   Or not at all ☐

19: In the last week, have YOU excluded other students from a group of friends or from joining in activities?

A lot ☐   A bit ☐   Or not at all ☐

20: In the last week, have YOU made other students give you their money or personal possessions?

A lot ☐   A bit ☐   Or not at all ☐

21: In the last week, have YOU threatened to hit, kick or use any form of violence against other students?

A lot ☐   A bit ☐   Or not at all ☐

22: In the last week, have YOU hit, kicked or used any form of violence against other students?

A lot ☐   A bit ☐   Or not at all ☐

23: Have you ever carried a weapon to school?   Yes ☐   No ☐

24: If you do bad things at school, who do you tell?

No one   ☐
A friend or girlfriend or boyfriend   ☐
A peer supporter   ☐
A member of your family   ☐
A teacher or other adult at school   ☐
Other   ☐

25: What are your suggestions for making your school a better place?

_____

_____

SECTION 5: ABOUT YOU

26: How old are you?   _____ years

27: Are you a boy or girl?

Boy ☐   Girl ☐

SCHOOL CLIMATE CHECKLIST (SECONDARY VERSION)
(adapted from Myers and Hutson, unpublished)

Please answer the following questions. There are no right or wrong answers; we want to know your thoughts. All of your answers will be treated confidentially, and will not be seen by anyone else at your school. Thank you for your help.

SECTION 1: WHERE YOU LIVE

1: Is the area where you live a nice place to be?

Yes ☐   No ☐

2: Who do you think is responsible for making the area where you live a nice place to be?
Please tick all that apply

Me	☐
Other young people	☐
Parents	☐
Other adults	☐
Local government/Council	☐

3: Please indicate how much you agree or disagree with the following statements about your local area …

	Agree	Disagree
The area is a friendly place to be	☐	☐
The area is a place where people look after each other	☐	☐
Most people in this area trust one other	☐	☐
There are lots of people in this area that I don't know	☐	☐
The area is unfriendly	☐	☐

SECTION 2: YOUR JOURNEY TO SCHOOL

4: Approximately how far away from your home is school?

Less than half an hour ☐   Half an hour or more ☐   An hour or more ☐

5: How safe do you feel travelling to and from school?

Very safe	☐
Fairly safe	☐
A bit unsafe	☐
Very unsafe	☐

SECTION 3: YOUR SCHOOL

6: Is school a nice place to be?

Yes ☐   No ☐

7: Who do you think is responsible for making the school a nice place to be?

Please tick all that apply

Me ☐

Other pupils ☐

Teachers ☐

Parents ☐

Other adults ☐

Local government/Council ☐

8: Please indicate how much you agree or disagree with the following statements about your school …

	Agree	**Disagree**
The school is a friendly place to be	☐	☐
The school is a place where people look after each other	☐	☐
Most people in this school trust one other	☐	☐
There are lots of people in this school that I don't know	☐	☐
The school is unfriendly	☐	☐

9: Have you ever played truant from school?

Yes ☐   No ☐

10: Have you ever been suspended or excluded from school?

Yes ☐   No ☐

11: How safe do you feel in the school toilets?

Very safe ☐   Fairly safe ☐   A bit unsafe ☐   Very unsafe ☐

12: How safe do you feel in the corridors (for example, when going between lessons)?

Very safe ☐   Fairly safe ☐   A bit unsafe ☐   Very unsafe ☐

13: How safe do you feel in lessons?

Very safe ☐   Fairly safe ☐   A bit unsafe ☐   Very unsafe ☐

14: How safe do you feel in the school playground?

Very safe ☐   Fairly safe ☐   A bit unsafe ☐   Very unsafe ☐

15: Where do you feel least safe and why?

16: Where do you feel most safe and why?

SECTION 4: NEGATIVE EXPERIENCES AT SCHOOL

17: Do you worry about being bullied at school?

A lot ☐   A bit ☐   Or not at all ☐

18: Are you worried about being rejected or disliked by your friends?

A lot ☐   A bit ☐   Or not at all ☐

19: In the last week, have you been threatened or intimidated in any way by anybody in this school?

A lot ☐   A bit ☐   Or not at all ☐

20: In the last week, has anyone stolen or damaged anything of yours at school?

Yes ☐   No ☐

21: When bad things happen, do you tell anyone?

Yes ☐   No ☐

22: If 'yes', who did you tell?

No one ☐
A friend or girlfriend or boyfriend ☐
A peer supporter ☐
A member of your family ☐
A teacher or other adult at school ☐
Other ☐

23: In the last week, have YOU upset other students by calling them hurtful names?

A lot ☐   A bit ☐   Or not at all ☐

24: In the last week, have YOU excluded other students from a group of friends or from joining in activities?

A lot ☐   A bit ☐   Or not at all ☐

25: In the last week, have YOU made other students give you their money or personal possessions?

A lot ☐   A bit ☐   Or not at all ☐

26: In the last week, have YOU threatened to hit, kick or use any form of violence against other students?

A lot ☐   A bit ☐   Or not at all ☐

27: In the last week, have YOU hit, kicked or used any form of violence against other students?

A lot ☐   A bit ☐   Or not at all ☐

28: Have you ever carried a weapon at school?

Yes ☐   No ☐

29: If you do bad things at school, who do you tell?

No one   ☐
A friend or girlfriend or boyfriend   ☐
A peer supporter   ☐
A member of your family   ☐
A teacher or other adult at school   ☐
Other   ☐

30: What are your suggestions for making your school a better place?

_____

_____

SECTION 5: ABOUT YOU

31: How old are you?   _____years

32: Are you a boy or girl?

Boy ☐   Girl ☐

References

Alderson, P. and Morrow, V. (2004) *Ethics, Social Research and Consulting with Children and Young People*. Ilford: Barnardo's.

Antidote (2003) *The Emotional Literacy Handbook: Processes, Practices and Resources to Promote Emotional Literacy*. London: David Fulton.

Arora, C.M.J. and Thompson, D.A. (1999) 'My life in school checklist', in N. Frederickson and R.J. Cameron (series eds) and S. Sharp (vol. ed.), *Bullying Behaviour in Schools: Psychology in Education Portfolio*. Windsor: NFER NELSON.

Aynsley-Green, A. (2006) *Bullying Today*. Office of the Children's Commissioner, www.childrenscommissioner.org/documents/bullying%20today%20(november%202006).pdf

Barter, C., Renold, E., Berridge, D. and Cawson, C. (2004) *Peer Violence in Children's Residential Care*. London: Palgrave Macmillan.

Beinart, S., Anderson, B., Lee, S. and Utting, D. (2002) *Youth at Risk? A National Survey of Risk Factors, Protective Factors and Problem Behaviour Among Young People in England, Scotland and Wales*. London: Joseph Rowntree Foundation.

Bergeron, N. and Schneider, B.H. (2005) 'Explaining cross-national differences in peer-directed aggression: a quantitative synthesis', *Aggressive Behavior*, 31(2): 116–37.

Boulton, M.J. (1995) 'Playground behaviour and peer interaction patterns of primary school boys classified as bullies, victims and not involved', *British Journal of Developmental Psychology*, 12, 315–29.

Cameron, L. and Thorsborne, M. (2001) 'Restorative justice and school discipline: mutually exclusive?', in H. Strang and J. Braithwaite (eds), *Restorative Justice and Civil Society*. Cambridge: Cambridge University Press. pp. 180–94.

Carter, C. (2002) 'Schools ethos and the construction of masculine identity: do schools create, condone and sustain aggression?', *Educational Review*, 54(1): 27–36.

Clark, A. (2004) 'The Mosaic approach and young children', in V. Lewis, M. Kellett, C. Robinson, S. Fraser and S. Dix (eds), *The Reality of Research with Children and Young People* (pp.142–56). London: Sage Publications.

Cole, T. (2000) *Kids Helping Kids*. Victoria, BC: Peer Resources.

Committee for Children (2002) *Second Step: A Violence Prevention Curriculum*. Seattle, WA: Author.

Cowie, H. and Jennifer, D. et al. (2007) *School Bullying and Violence: Taking*

Action. University of Surrey. www.vista-europe.org

Cowie, H., Naylor, P., Rivers, I., Smith, P.K. and Pereira, B. (2002) 'Measuring workplace bullying. Aggressive and Violent Behaviour', 7, 33–51.

Cowie, H., and Sharp, S. (1994) 'How to tackle bullying through the curriculum', in S. Sharp and P.K. Smith (eds), *Tackling Bullying in Your School.* London: Routledge. pp. 41–78.

Cowie, H. and Wallace, P. (2000) *Peer Support in Action: From Bystanding to Standing By.* London: Sage Publications.

Cowie, H., Boardman, C., Dawkins, J. and Jennifer, D. (2004) *Emotional Health and Well-Being: A Practical Guide for Schools.* London: Sage Publications.

Department for Education and Skills (DfES) (2003). *Every Child Matters.* Green Paper. London: Department for Skills and Education.

Department for Education and Skills (2004) *Every Child Matters: Change for Children in Schools.* Copies are available to download from http://publications.teachernet.gov.uk/eOrderingDownload/DfES-1089-2004.pdf

Department of Health (2004) *Promoting Emotional Health and Well-Being Through the National Healthy School Standard.* London: HMSO.

Derrington, C. and Kendall, S. (2004) *Gypsy Traveller Students in Secondary Schools: Culture, Identity and Achievement.* Nottingham: Trentham Books.

European Charter for Democratic Schools Without Violence (2004) www.coe.int/t/e/integrated_projects/democracy/02_activities/15_european_school_charter/04_Charter.asp#TopOfPage

Farrington, D. (1996) *Understanding and Preventing Youth Crime.* York: York Publishing Services for the Joseph Rowntree Foundation.

Frey, K.S., Nolen, S.B., Van Schoiack Edstrom, L. and Hirschstein, M.K. (2005) 'Effects of a school-based social-emotional competence program: linking children's goals, attributions, and behavior', *Applied Developmental Psychology*, 26: 171–200.

Galvin, P. (2006) 'The role of a school audit in preventing and minimizing violence', in C. Gittins (ed.), *Violence Reduction in Schools – How to Make a Difference.* Strasbourg: Council of Europe Publishing. pp. 23–38.

Goleman, D. (1996) *Emotional Intelligence: Why It Can Matter More Than IQ.* London: Bloomsbury.

Grossman, D.C., Neckerman, H.J., Koepsell, T.D., Liu, P.Y., Asher, K.N., Beland, K., Frey, K. and Rivara, F.P. (1997) 'Effectiveness of a violence prevention curriculum among children in elementary school: a randomized controlled trial', *Journal of the American Medical Association*, 277: 1605–11.

Gulbenkian Foundation (1995) *Children and Violence: The Report of the Commission on Children and Violence.* London: Calouste Gulbenkain Foundation.

Haddon, A., Goodman, H., Park, J. and Crick, R.D. (2005) 'Evaluating emotional literacy in schools: the development of the School Emotional Environment for Learning Survey', *Pastoral Care in Education*, 23(4): 5–16.

Hill, M., Laybourn, A. and Borland, M. (1996) 'Engaging with primary-aged children about their emotions and well-being: methodological considerations', *Children and Society*, 10(2): 129–44.

Hutson, N. and Cowie, H. (in press) Setting up an email peer support service, *Pastoral Care in Education.*

Hutson, N. and Myers, C. (unpublished) *School Climate Checklist* (primary version)

Jennifer, D. and Shaughnessy, J. (2005) 'Promoting non-violence in schools: the role of cultural, organizational and managerial factors, *Educational and Child Psychology*, 22(3): 58–66.

Maines, B. and Robinson, G. (1997) *Crying for Help: The No Blame Approach to Bullying*. Bristol: Lucky Duck Publishing.

Mauthner, M. (1997) 'Methodological aspects of collecting data from children: lessons from three research projects', Children and Society, 11: 16–28.

Mayer, J.D. and Salovey, P. (1997) 'What is emotional intelligence?', in P. Salovey and D.J. Sluyter (eds), *Emotional Development and Emotional Intelligence*. New York: Basic Books, www.unh.edu/emotional_intelligence/EIAssets/Emotional IntelligenceProper/EI1997MSWhatIsEI.pdf

Mencap (2000) *Living in Fear*. London: Mencap.

Meuret, D. and Morlaix, S. (2003) 'Conditions of success of a school's self-evaluation: some lessons of a European experience', *School Effectiveness and School Improvement*, 14(1): 53–71.

Morrison, B. (2003) Regulating safe school communities: being responsive and restorative, *Journal of Educational Administration*, 41(6): 689–704.

Myers, C. and Hutson, N. (unpublished) *School Climate Checklist* (secondary version)

Noret, N. and Rivers, I. (2006) 'The prevalence of bullying by text message and email: results of a four year study', poster session presented at the BPS Annual Conference, Cardiff, UK, March.

Ólafsson, R.F. and Jóhannsdóttir, H.L. (2004) 'Coping with bullying in the workplace: the effect of gender, age and type of bullying', *British Journal of Guidance and Counselling*, 32(3), 319–33.

Oliver, C. and Candappa, M. (2003) *Tackling Bullying: Listening to the Views of Children and Young People*. Research Report RR400. London: DfES Publications.

Olweus, D. (1996) *The Revised Olweus Bully/Victim Questionnaire*. Bergen: Research Center for Health Promotion (HEMIL Center), University of Bergen.

Olweus, D. (1999) 'Sweden', in P.K. Smith, Y. Morita, J. Junger-Tas, D. Olweus, R. Catalano and P. Slee (eds), *The Nature of School Bullying*. London: Routledge. pp. 7–27.

Pretty, J.N., Guijt, I., Thompson, J. and Scoones, I. (1995) *Participatory Learning in Action: A Trainer's Guide*. IIED Participatory Methodology Series. London: International Institute for Environment and Development.

Punch, S. (2002) 'Research with children: the same or different from research with adults?', *Childhood*, 9(3), 321–41.

Rigby, K. and McLaughlin, C. (2005) 'Bystander behaviour and bullying', *Special issue: Pastoral Care in Education*, 23(22): 1–3.

Riley, P.L. and Segal, E.C. (2002) 'Preparing to evaluate a school violence prevention program: Students Against Violence Everywhere (SAVE)', *Journal of School Violence*, 1(2): 73–86.

Rivers, I. and Cowie, H. (2006) Bullying and homophobia at UK schools: a perspective on factors affecting and recovery, *Journal of Gay and Lesbian Issues in Education*, 3(4): 11–43.

Robson, S. (1996). 'Home and school: a potentially powerful partnership', in S. Robson and S. Smedley (eds), *Education in Early Childhood: First Things First*. London: David Fulton. pp. 56–74.

Robbins, S.P. (1994) Essentials of Organisational Behaviour. New Jersey: Prentice Hall International.

Roffey, S. (2000) 'Addressing bullying in schools: organisational factors from policy to practice', *Educational and Child Psychology*, 17(1): 6–19.

Salmivalli, C., Lagerspetz, K., Björkqvist, K., Österman, K. and Kaukiainen, A. (1996) 'Bullying as a group process: participant roles and their relations to social status within the group', *Aggressive Behavior*, 20: 1–15.

Salovey, P. and Mayer, J. (1990) 'Emotional intelligence', *Imagination, Cognition and Personality*, 9: 185–211.

Sammons, P., Hillman, J. and Mortimore, P. (1995) *Key Characteristics of Effective Schools*. London: Institute of Education/Office for Standards in Education.

Shariff, S. (2005) 'Cyber-dilemmas in the new millennium: balancing free expression and student safety in cyber-space', special issue: Schools and Courts: Competing Rights in the New Millennium, *McGill Journal of Education*, 40(3): 467–87.

Sharp, S., Arora, T., Smith, P.K. and Whitney, I. (1994) 'How to measure bullying in your school', in P.K. Smith and S. Sharp (eds), *Tackling Bullying in Your School*. pp. 8–21.

Sharp, S. and Smith, P.K. (1994) *Tackling Bullying in Your School: A Practical Handbook for Teachers*. London: Routledge.

Sharpe, P. (2001) *Nurturing Emotional Literacy*. London: David Fulton.

Shaughnessy, J. (2006) 'Creating a school climate of convivencia through whole-school policies', in C. Gittins (ed.), *Violence Reduction in Schools – How to Make a Difference*. Strasbourg: Council of Europe Publishing. pp. 39–49.

Smith, P.K. and Levan, S. (1995) 'Perceptions and experiences of bullying in younger pupils', *British Journal of Educational Psychology*, 65: 489–500.

Smith, P.K., Howard, S. and Thompson, F. (2007) 'Use of the Support Group method to tackle bullying', *Pastoral Care in Education*, 25(2): 4–13.

Sullivan, K. (2000) *The Anti-Bullying Handbook*. Oxford: Oxford University Press.

Sullivan, K., Cleary, M. and Sullivan, G. (2004) *Bullying in Secondary Schools*. London: Paul Chapman Publishing.

United Nations (1989). *Convention on the Rights of the Child*. Innocenti Studies, Florence: UNICEF.

United Nations Children's Fund (UNICEF) (2007) *Child Poverty in Perspective: An Overview of Child-Well-being in Rich Countries*. Innocenti Report Card 7. Florence: UNICEF Innocenti Research Centre.

Van Schoiack Edstrom, L., Frey, K.S. and Beland, K. (2002) 'Changing adolescents' attitudes about relational and physical aggression: an early evaluation of a school-based intervention', *School Psychology Review*, 31(2): 201–16.

Varnava, G. (2000) *Towards a Non-Violent Society: Checkpoints for Schools*. London: National Children's Bureau.

Varnava, G. (2002) *Towards a Non-Violent Society: Checkpoints for Young People*. London: National Children's Bureau.

Wachtel, T. and McCold, T. (2001) 'Restorative justice in everyday life: beyond the formal ritual', in H. Strang and J. Braithwaite (eds), *Restorative Justice and Civil Society*. Cambridge: Cambridge University Press. pp. 114–29.

Weare, K. (2004) *Developing the Emotionally Literate School*. London: Paul Chapman Publishing.

Weare, K. and Gray, G. (2003) What Works in Developing Children's Emotional and Social Competence and Wellbeing? DfES Research Report 456. London: DfES.

Wilson, D., Sharp, C. and Patterson, A. (2006) *Young People and Crime: Findings from the 2005 Offending, Crime and Justice Survey*. London: Research Development and Statistics Directorate, Home Office.

World Health Organization (WHO) (2002) *World Report on Violence and Health*. Geneva: World Health Organization.

Young, S. (1998) 'The support group approach to bullying in schools', *Educational Psychology in Practice*, 14: 32–9.

Young, S. and Holdorf, G. (2003) 'Using solution focused brief therapy in individual referrals for bullying', *Educational Psychology in Practice*, 19: 271–82.

Young Women's Christian Association (YWCA) (2004) 'Pride not prejudice: young lesbian and bisexual women', YWCA Briefing, www.ywca-gb.org.uk/briefings.asp

Youth Justice Board (YJB) (2004) *National Evaluation of the Restorative Justice in Schools Programme*. London: Youth Justice Board, www.youth-justice-board.gov.uk.

Youth Justice Board (YJB) (2005) *Risk and Protective Factors*. London: Youth Justice Board, www.youth-justice-board.gov.uk.

Index